THE GAME CHANGER

A NOVEL

MARC BONA

SKIP
THANKS FOR
THE AMAZING
EDIT!

LUMINARE PRESS

WWW.LUMINAREPRESS.COM

The Game Changer
© 2018 Marc Bona

Printed in the United States of America

Cover Illustration by Kathy Hagedorn
Cover Design by Melissa Lund

Luminare Press
438 Charnelton St., Suite 101
Eugene, OR 97401
www.luminarepress.com

LCCN: 2018945944
ISBN: 978-1-944733-83-4

For Lynne

TABLE OF CONTENTS

PROLOGUE

In the future, the game had changed. The money and the pressure and the American way of being—needing one final champion—gave way to a playoff system in college football. Many thought the playoff system would finalize a champion and that would be the end of it. Far from it. It simply ignited another level that widened the gap between colleges and, well, football schools.

Twelve new colleges grew from the playoff system. Pressure mounted from everyone—media, fans, even the colleges themselves—to be left with one undisputed champion. The old bowl system slowly became a shell of itself. A new system took root, all because two comparable teams who won their bowl games and played in equally competitive leagues wasn't enough. The leagues had merged and morphed so many times only a handful remained. The demand was there: You couldn't go through a season as a player, practicing and playing and working and be left with doubt. You couldn't go through the year as a fan and not know who the champ was. The arguments were fun, but in the end they weren't enough. Everyone needed closure. The polls, who were determined by humans for decades, were given over entirely to computers and algorithms, which despite precise calculations of all sorts of variables, from the weather to the average weight of offensive linemen, didn't do any better than the flesh and blood quantifiers. So the humans took them back.

Changes in the professional game had evolved slowly. The National Pro League trickled out its changes, with a rabid fan base and advanced technology playing as big a role as anything else by 2028. The league's popularity dipped when concussions became a near epidemic, but medical advancements and better helmet sensors helped ease fears. The real salve, though, came when the league tied penalties to money. Lead with your head, get tossed from the game, pay with your wallet. The added twist of the knife, though, hurt the teams' payroll. Illegal, vicious hits knocked off how much they could spend on the draft.

Media hype and national frenzy pushed the league's season opener into a near holiday. Networks not contracted to broadcast games ran everything else: Interviews with players, historic highlights and, of course, countless hours of analysis. One network prided itself on showing more statistics than interviews.

The games had long ago gone to pay-per-view—first on a trial basis, then gradually games were added until the entire season, playoffs and championship were shown via pay-per-view.

It was when pay-per-view finished broadcasting its first championship that the league truly came into its own 21st century identity. The season stretched from late August preseason to mid-February. Preseason games were cut from four to three—teams stayed home for one game, went on the road for one game and played in a neutral site for one. The latter aimed to get the game to parts of the country that didn't have a pro stadium nearby but had decent population centers—Cheyenne, Wyoming; Amarillo, Texas; Louisville,

Kentucky. "Neutral-site" parties were held in these and other mid-sized cities, generating fervor like the Super Bowl. The players loved it because they were paid as if they had played four games. The only grumbling came from coaches, who had one fewer game to evaluate second- and third-string talent.

The all-star game, pitting the league's best two weeks after the championship, had been scrapped. It had always been more important simply to be named to the team, but playing it never was a big deal. "Teams" weren't really teams, and few fans ever recalled stats or plays from the game. The league claimed it dropped the game because teams feared injury to a star player, but the real reason was because it wasn't generating as much advertising revenue as hoped. Still, the NPL sent the honorees and their families to Hawaii for a week's vacation.

In its place a "Fans Game" was added. Fans would vote for the game in the playoffs they were hoping to see. It turned out to be a win-win situation for the league. If the teams ended up meeting in the postseason, the league had confirmation of a big viewing audience, allowing for increased advertising rates. If it didn't materialize, league officials considered putting the teams in the following season's debut game. Fans had a voice. And the league had their contact information and demographics.

The sport's popularity grew even when it seemed like there wasn't room to grow. It wasn't only the pay-per-view channels that were making money off professional football. When Las Vegas added small-college games to its betting line, the league publicly balked because of its anti-gambling stance. But it turns out there were many Americans who attended small colleges or who lived near them, and they wanted to be able to have a few bucks riding on their alma mater.

Fantasy leagues of years past had emphasized the performance of position-players rather than the team as a whole. But the next phase of fan involvement came when the stock market jumped in. The Players Exchange—or PLX—created a financial system where investors could buy a share of a player. Their value was reflected in stock price, which fluctuated on performance of players and teams. Because the PLX included penny stocks only, no one was retiring on their earnings, but it was an affordable option. The player received a small percentage based on shares held. The money went directly to their retirement fund. The more likable a player was, the more people wanted a piece of him.

Slowly the diehards were phased out of attendance because of exorbitant ticket prices. Turnstiles electronically registered fans. Giant, plush leather recliners were added to the first few rows in stadiums, with an electronic keypad to have food and drink delivered from concessions, billed directly to credit cards on file. Most stadiums were domes. The few that weren't had Plexiglas overhangs on the expensive seats with small heaters or mini-air-conditioner units because, after all, who wants to be uncomfortable watching a game? All that cost money, and for the most part only companies could afford the seats.

And then there was the virtual-reality money. Teams sold fitted helmet-like goggles with their logos on each side to fans all over the country. Like Chicago's team but were out of town? No problem. Bring your goggles and pony up for a "seat." Retired to Florida but wanted to follow New York? Turn up the air conditioning at home, put on the helmet goggles, and enjoy the game. Fans paid by vantage—

one price to watch from the nosebleed seats, while another, pricier option allowed them to "sit" on the bench. Every spot in a stadium was valued; there were no limits on seats by vantage. So an infinite number of fans from Phoenix to Philadelphia could watch from the same 50-yard-line seat. Who wouldn't want 360-degree live-streaming capability? Of course, for years the league had looked to Europe to expand, and did so with teams in London and Frankfurt. A new Concord-like plane had been developed, and served as the league's charter. The European teams played "two and twos," meaning they would travel to the United States to compete in back-to-back Sunday games, then home for two. The league continued to expand slowly. The plane's construction maintained the narrow design of the old Concord, which did a lot for aerodynamics but little for team camaraderie, since everyone sat alone. Players listened to music on the barely five-hour flight. Teams hired nutritionists and scientists to study jet lag with the hopes of easing players' bodies back into routines as quickly as possible.

Gone were the classic stadium names of years past. Almost every stadium and field included commercial branding in its name. Fail-Safe Stadium, named for an insurance company, and Randall Field, named after a hardware chain, for instance, became home to Boston's team. Season-ticket holders also received a slight discount at that particular company. If a company went out of business or did not want to continue the deal, another was waiting to take its place in the giant marquees that hung over the arches or walkway or gate. Parking-lot locations were not labeled "orange" or "blue" or whatever the team colors were, but rather a sponsor's name. Everything was a money-making opportunity. Even the back of goal posts had logos on them.

Players couldn't see them and they didn't interfere with the game, but every camera caught them.

The changes on the field, in a way, were even greater than the ones off of it.

The officials' subjective nature of where to spot the ball on goal-line plays no longer was an issue. A microchip was implanted in the ball, with sensors lighting a small receiver attached to the line judge's belt. If the ball crossed the plane but could not be seen because a scrum of players crumpled together, the official would know. Multiple camera angles merely checked to make sure the ball carrier wasn't down first. The "chain gang" measuring first downs became a thing of the past, too. The ball's chip measured precisely on the field where it was. A light on the scoreboard—usually sponsored by a local utility—would flash a giant "TD" or "FD" for first down, prompting the usual chorus of cheers or boos.

It was considered revolutionary when teams used coaches to take instant pictures from hand-held cameras in the press box to show the opposing team's defensive setups. That process, which took minutes to shoot, develop and run down to the field, became instantaneous with digital photography. Coaches and players on the sidelines could see immediately what defenses were planning and who exactly was on the field.

Players, of course, had grown bigger and faster. Dietitians and nutritionists watched players in the off-season, to monitor weight and stress on the heart, especially for linemen. The natural grass offered some protection, but when 300-pound bodies slam into each other play after play, like two small buses colliding on a city street, injuries are bound to happen.

Despite the technology and extensive support staff and college farm system and all the money, in the end it was still the same game played decades earlier. One team had to advance the ball over the goal line, and the other had to stop them.

PART I

MEDIA DAY

CHAPTER 1

There really wasn't anything more to do than to let the plan play out.

The smallish man stood like a tailor, smoothing the large figure's golf shirt that really didn't need any smoothing. The two remained quiet as the older man brushed invisible lint off the shirt, lost in his world of thinking, carefully going over his mental checklist of what needed to be done to put the plan in place.

"You look strong and healthy," he said. "Strong and healthy."

A slight smile faced the older man, but no words.

The older man continued smoothing, even brushing the khakis of the much bigger frame, who stayed quiet, unmoving. The checklist continued in his head, interrupted only by occasional thoughts of his dream, how long it had taken to get to this moment. The initial idea had come to him in a dream in college. He had worked in his spare time. He had turned down offers of advancement at work knowing a move up the ladder would eat into his precious time with his nephew. Then the engineering came, and that made the laboring of the design seem easy. The years he worked with his ideas had been challenging and taken all his creative strength and engineering know-how. But the engineering part was, well, it took "challenging" to new heights.

"I think, as we say, you will 'knock them dead,' " the older man said, with just a wisp of Eastern European lilt in his voice. "You will be the hit, the star."

The apartment had notes strewn and tools scattered, but little in the way of furniture. At best, a stranger would have considered it sparse. At worst, dingy and depressing.

He continued brushing, then he stopped, and faced Riga Rotinom.

They were ready.

CHAPTER 2

Brooks Scranton looked out from his offices adjacent to Emerald Lake Stadium as occasional cars and vans rolled into the media lot. The driver-less vehicles were quiet, silently slipping into the gated area. Players already were in the locker room, catching up and getting what he liked to call "T and T"—treatments and tape. He watched silently, his own preseason routine of sorts. His mind wandered as he glanced over the piers across Lake Erie, the occasional whitecap whipping up on the horizon. He was a rare breed of an owner—a maverick, but not only in that he was unpredictable and tough to figure out at times. He had made his money through a start-up venture he took online years earlier. He sold it, and while other executives might have taken the proceeds to retire and sail the world, Scranton invested. He found boring projects and buildings and trusts, sinking money in at the right times. What he didn't do was make headlines. What he did was make money. And he took the profits and realized a dream: Owning a professional football team.

He made his move for the Cleveland Stormcats when their value was low and there were no takers; the team had come off four losing seasons and the city had fought the previous owners on their request for financing a new stadium.

Then Scranton came in, and when he said he wouldn't use a dime of public money to finance construction of a stadium, well, the city embraced him faster than blitzing defensive backs launching after a quarterback. It was a tough city, one steeled in long-disappeared manufacturing jobs. That had changed, of course, but the residents still prided themselves on being tough—tough enough to remain one of the few cities without a domed stadium. And until now, the stadium was one of only a few with no company's name attached. Scranton would wait for the right time on that. He was a patient man.

Brooks Scranton was known not to grab the spotlight from his players; he would come down to the lockers only after losses, in a kind of father-figure way, consoling his kids after losing their Little League game, the dad who would take the kids for ice cream or pizza and then everything would be all right. He vowed he would never show up after a win, and he never did. He thought players were the ones who earned the "W" on the field, and he would not steal their glory. He held the rarified vantage as a players' owner.

He formed his opinion of a player's ability and heart from practices more so than from games. Watching football practice is about as exciting as watching someone mix ingredients for a cake. Players stretch and generally get ready together, then are broken into smaller units who run the same drills over and over and over.

Scranton loved it. There was something calming about it. When they went to two-a-days he'd get to work early, then as players hit the field he would move from his desk to a loveseat by the window, drinking coffee and watching his boys. He'd study body language, how they reacted with teammates and coaches. When they broke for lunch, he would hit the weights, his own workout, or run, then it was back to the office. The faint whish whish whish of the sprinklers whirring outside after practice always calmed him.

Today's routine was altered only a little. He had one appointment on his schedule—meeting Dr. Janis Daugava.

The team's behind-the-scenes staff had been busy making sure everything was in place for this day, the beginning of a season that had media members, fans and the team feeling confident—not cocky, but confident that pieces were in place. Coaches had been at a feverish pace working on the draft, watching films, evaluating players, reading reports. Today was the beginning of all that work.

The media slowly began setting up along the sidelines. Cameras were stationed and reporters mingled. The old print-only guard dwindled year by year. Tape recorders were a thing of the past. Cameras got smaller, and the PDRs—Personal Digital Recorders—outnumbered handheld notebooks. PDRs allowed recording but also transcribed words—even those almost mumbled—on a small, clear screen. A reporter could post an account much quicker by simply moving the transcribed quotes into what they were putting online. Editors didn't edit so much as they scrambled to get their reporters' stories onto as many social platforms as possible. The devices took smart-phone technology to another level. The memory was enormous. They were designed by a former newspaper photographer with a bent for technology. Everything, in the world of football and the media, was about speed.

When it came to speed on the field, Reilly Carver was it. He was one of the first to come out of the tunnel, his introduction booming across the mostly empty stadium. It was Scranton's idea to introduce the players this year to the media, treating the day like a grand event, like a game or, more realistically, a recruiting event to get the media on board.

"AT RUNNING BACK, NUMBER 21, REILLY CARVER!" boomed the public-address announcer over the field. "AT FULLBACK, NUMBER 34, BRONX THOMAS! And on and on the hokey introductions went.

Carver—half Irish, half Black—hailed from the smallest high school in Iowa. At first, few noticed him as a top college prospect, but his scampering through defenses led him to Minnesota Southern, one of the dozen football factories that grew from the playoff system instituted years earlier. He fought his way up the depth chart, and when he was finished, he owned the all-time touchdown record at Minnesota Southern.

Media Day was an annual ritual, held at almost every college and professional team. If you were a player, it was a light assignment. If you were there with a uniform on, you had made the team. Everyone was on good graces. Players wore clean, pressed uniforms, waiting for reporters to approach and chat with them about every aspect of their upcoming season. It was an important time for the media, especially those from smaller markets, because quotes gathered here weren't used only for that day's post. They were saved for future stories. It was a chance to bank a lot of notes and quotes and eat a usually pretty good buffet.

The sun beat down on players milling about as the media filtered in. Players would be available on the field, as would doctors, trainers and other front-office staff, for reporters and broadcasters to surround and probe. They looked like doctors trying to learn from a patient with a rare disease.

Dunwoody Culpepper watched the reporters across the field watching the players. The 6-foot, 5-inch tight end had not drawn much attention in the NPL until a year ago, his third season, when he caught a personal-best 24 catches for four touchdowns. Not every player in the league came out of the factories, like Carver. Culpepper went to the University of Georgia, a big strong suburban kid who loved the game and worked at it. Next to him was Thomas, a fullback from a burg just outside of New York City, and Pun Wisgenti, a lanky receiver who had turned in a quiet but solid rookie season. Pun was a rare breed in the NPL, because he probably was the only player who actually had studied engineering at a small, western Pennsylvania college, and had graduated. He had an odd sense of humor in the locker room ("Everything was going smoothly at the bakery until they made pumpernickel bread. Then everything went awry") that usually just drew surprised faces that crinkled, teammates trying to figure out what he was saying. Pun never laughed at his own jokes, and neither did his teammates. He shared a love of the game, born from playing pickup games in the cul-de-sac where he grew up. He just happened to be one of those players who broke the dumb-jock stereotype.

Carver joined them, as did Brock McAdams, an offensive lineman with a cropped head of hair that looked like a barber spent all of two minutes cutting. His head was like an upside-down brush. They faced the reporters coming across in a slow advance.

"Yo, DC," Bronx said as he touched hands with Culpepper. "Get a little tan there in those Georgia woods man? You get fat barbecuing over the summer?"

"Hey," said the square-shouldered Culpepper, smiling at his teammate.

"Hey man," Carver chuckled. "What do you eat while you're tucked in that thar cabin—'that thar'—isn't that how you folks talk down there?"

Wisgenti twanged out the first few notes of "Dueling Banjos."

"It's a house, dude, in the suburbs," said Culpepper. "We ain't going out in the woods for no good reason."

"I heard you were choppin' down trees, man, lighting up that chainsaw," McAdams said.

"I don't own a chainsaw," Culpepper said, defending the ribbing. "I may hunt, but I don't chop down trees."

"No, of course not," Wisgenti said. "He pays someone to clear the trees."

"At number 80, Dunwoody Tree-chopper, Tree-chopper!" Carver said in announcer voice.

It was Thomas who saw the two men, one much more than a foot taller than the smaller one, about 40 yards away. The larger figure appeared to be walking with a child.

"What in the hell is that?"

The players' banter stopped as they stared at the unlikely pair downfield.

Walking toward the players was a diminutive, neatly dressed man in a beige sports coat, bowler and crisp, white Oxford and dark pants. But it was the other man who caught the players' attention.

Wisgenti: "He's gotta be seven, easily."

Culpepper: "He's topping that. That thing is seven-four. Freakin' Andre the Giant proportions."

No one laughed. Coming at them was someone none of them had seen. He dwarfed the older man, whose head barely came up to the big man's ribs.

"That's a lot of beef," Thomas said. "That guy's gotta go

four bills, easily. Hate to have to move him around."

"Hate to get moved around by him," Carver added.

No one knew this guy. More importantly, no one knew if he were offense or defense.

The pair stopped near the end zone and questioned a groundskeeper, who pointed toward the press box and then the tunnel. The old man doffed his bowler and the two turned. The large man, in khakis and golf shirt, stood motionless for a second as he glanced at the players. Then he turned and walked with the smaller man.

The players stared back, speechless.

CHAPTER 3

Catharine Payton Andrews looked down as she carefully stepped across the out-of-bounds chalk, neatly lined for Media Day. It was an old habit, a minor superstition she had kept since she was a girl playing softball. In college she always stepped over the line on her way to shortstop. She never knew why, it just seemed like the right thing to do. She thought briefly of the times she'd step onto the dirt of a well-placed diamond, raked and smoothed over. Before warm-up tosses, she would watch the slight swirls of dust blow across the granules of dirt on the infield.

A puff of chalk clouding around her brought her back to reality, as a lumpy cameraman who she didn't recognize stepped right on the chalk line next to her.

"All right, they say this is the year," he barked. But she knew the introduction would come next. The guy was angling for a compatriot among his media brethren, someone to bounce a rumor off of, someone to ask 'hey, who made that play?' or other double-check. Andrews didn't mind helping people, but she also thought you do your homework before covering a game. Too many of her colleagues didn't.

She buried her head in her PDR and picked up her pace, leaving the cameraman behind as she walked to the 40-yard line to the small group of offensive players.

At five feet, four inches, most of her colleagues and all the players on the field towered over her. Her short dark hair fell above the starched white button-down she wore, its only wrinkles coming from the shoulder strap of her satchel. Her khakis and dark loafers finished off what she considered her "uniform" for work most days. She wore sunglasses but had managed to get through life without needing glasses, though she figured it was a matter of time after all the hours she spent glaring into laptop screens and PDRs.

Andrews was one of several reporters who covered the Cleveland Stormcats on a regular basis for The American, an international sports publication. Like football, sports-writing had changed.

No one wrote a prototypical game story anymore. A large online outfit in a major market would keep two or three reporters on a team, each contributing shorter bites on a variety of topics. Everything in a game was broken down. Fans demanded it. Andrews' specialty was medicine. If a player went down with an unusual injury, it was her job to investigate the injury, talk to doctors, find out the timetable for the player's return and sometimes explain it in a graphic or video for readers and viewers. She also wrote a short column about her observations of a game—turning points, key plays and other nuggets. Her colleague Dallas Trent focused on statistics, feeding the nation's obsession that had started years earlier when fantasy leagues were born. Fans knew him as "The Numbers Guy." He was known among colleagues as a bean counter.

The pack of reporters looked like a small, hesitant army advancing across a grassy verge. Andrews found her way to the group of offensive players. Broadcasters set up with a nod or "Hey, hot one today!"—anything to break the ice with a bunch of players who weren't totally thrilled to be there and had no desire to break the ice with anyone but each other or an attractive woman. Several broadcasters surrounded the quartet of quarterbacks near the 10-yard line, with a coach nearby. One was dropping back to pass, then holding his position, obviously posing for a photo. Other coaches huddled downfield. The defensive unit was split by position, the defensive backs talking to a kid from a local college and a radio guy. The linebackers stayed all business as reporters quizzed them on the past season, what they expected in terms of changing defenses—as if any of them knew at this point. The linemen were asked about weight training, and what set them apart from other teams. They were a chatty bunch, because once the season started they weren't quoted as often as quarterbacks and coaches. With linemen, there was a certain bravado you had to account for. They knew who did the job in the trenches, who opened the holes for the backs. The trainers sat on a sideline bench, talking with a TV cameraman. The punters and kickers were ignored.

Andrews scanned the players, seeking out Carver and Thomas, the backfield duo. She was working on a story about the specific wear and tear that the game took on running backs' knees, comparing players of today who competed on grass that grew even in domes to their counterparts from years ago who played on turf.

Carver saw her first. "Miss Andrews, how's life treating you?"

"Not bad, sir, ready for another season?"

"Always, bring the defenses on, bring 'em ON."

"Yeah, bring 'em on, baby," echoed McAdams, trying to

angle in to the interview. The backfield got all the attention. Andrews ignored him and got down to business.

"Reilly, as I said when I called, I am doing a story on knees—"

"Hey want to see my knees? McAdams broke in, trying to roll up his football pants.

"No, their whiteness might reflect the sun too much," Andrews said. The other players laughed.

"Doing a story on the procedures now, verses 20, 25 years ago," she continued to Carver.

"I didn't play 25 years ago."

Andrews smiled. Carver was being more quippy than difficult.

"And if you did, would you have preferred to play on all that turf they used?" she asked, segueing into the interview.

Carver smiled for a second, then got serious. "Tough to say. You trade a bit of speed for more injuries. The old turf, I heard when you got smeared across it, it cut you like someone took sandpaper to your body. Not to mention the fact that the older turf didn't give as much. The grass, yeah, it's more forgiving, but you lose that half-second or two."

"How important is that half-second in today's game?"

Carver glanced at the defensive unit, looking like wolves, hungry for dinner.

"It's important," he said sternly, his mind thinking back to when his left knee was scoped years earlier.

Andrews flipped a page and kept the questions coming. She still liked to use the old-fashioned notebooks in addition to her PDR. Carver was straight with his answers, didn't force jokes, didn't give her too much of a hard time.

"You've had surgery," she said. "Do you think about it often?"

"Only when you ask me about it," he said.

CHAPTER 4

As Andrews and the other reporters quizzed the play-ers on the warm day, Scranton split his time—reading coaches' reports, checking online news, and glancing out the window at the small enclaves of players and reporters grouped across the field. When his secretary buzzed him, his heart jumped for half a second. The man who was known for his business-like demeanor, a calming influence to those in his inner circle, actually was a little nervous.

"Dr. Daugava," said Scranton as the door opened and two figures walked through, the older, smaller man removing his hat and putting down his briefcase. Scranton learned quickly the doctor pronounced his name "duh-GOW-vuh." Once Scranton learned something, he rarely forgot it.

"Mr. Scranton, I trust you are well and the season will begin as you expect?"

Scranton stood and shook the doctor's hand.

"Yes, Doctor, we're almost ready. Today is a step in the direction we want to go."

The small man smiled, but Scranton didn't notice. He could not take his eyes off the larger figure.

"Mr. Scranton," Daugava said, "you remember my nephew, Riga Rotinom." Daugava pronounced the name ro-TIN-ohm as he gently tapped the large man with his hat.

Scranton stood silent. Rotinom looked at Daugava, who nodded, then slowly turned to Scranton, extending his hand.

"Sir," a low voice said.

When Scranton was 12 years old his parents sat him down and told him his mother had cancer and wasn't well. The next day the three of them drove to the hospital to meet with a doctor. When the physician turned to the boy, he stuck out his hand. Scranton shook it, felt his knees tremble and his palms sweat while the rest of him felt chilled. The doctor did little to ease the boy's nervousness. When they drove home later he swore to himself he would never be that nervous again when meeting a stranger, and he never was.

Until this moment.

"Please," said Scranton, gesturing to the couch. "Can I get you anything?"

"No, thank you," the doctor said, as he and Rotinom walked to the seating area near the windows.

The three sat, Scranton calming some but still amazed at what he was about to do, what was about to happen.

It was the usually introverted doctor who started the conversation.

"I trust nothing has changed since our last meeting?"

"No," said Scranton, finally turning his attention from Rotinom. "Nothing. Papers are ready. I have the standard league contract ready. You saw the draft, and nothing has been altered. I also have our agreement and your first check."

"And the physical examination—it is not a problem?" asked Daugava.

"No," Scranton said, clearing his voice. "The paperwork is signed, clean bill of health." He turned his attention back to Rotinom.

"How does he—"

"You may ask him yourself. He doesn't bite. Not even on the field; he knows the rules," Daugava said, smiling.

Scranton eased back in his chair, finally relaxing some. He still had so many questions, from the day Daugava called and suggested a meeting. Scranton thought the meeting was the doctor's way of gaining an entry to apply to be a team doctor or trainer, but it turned out to be anything but. Doc, as he liked to be called, simply said he wanted to talk about procedures to keep players healthy, but only with Scranton. Scranton remembered rolling his eyes and almost—almost—kicking him out when the conversation shifted and he told of his nephew who he deemed "a great football player." Scranton figured it was family pride. He had never heard of the nephew, never recalled his name on a scouting report. Then the doctor said the nephew had not gone to college. It was turning into a wasted meeting. But Doc had made a quiet, simple promise that Scranton would not be disappointed. Scranton wasn't sold, though, until the doctor showed him the video.

Rotinom lifting, Rotinom doing agility drills, Rotinom hitting and driving the sled. Rotinom facing a ball machine, reacting with lightning quick speed as he swatted would-be passes like King Kong knocking planes out of the air. The only drawback was not seeing him against other bodies. That meeting led to a subsequent one when he met the nephew, saw him in person to make sure the tapes weren't faked, and this wasn't all some big hoax. It wasn't. Riga Rotinom, at 7 feet, 4 inches, and 440 pounds, was as real as flesh and blood.

"I am still amazed, and stunned. Doc, not too many people get me feeling that way."

"Mr. Scranton, I guess I am used to it. It—this plan, the research—has been with me for many years. You see, my designs, my work, have taken so long, nothing shocks me. Riga has been with me a long time," he said, smiling at his nephew, who was staring out the window at the players below.

"I feel like a rookie coming out of the tunnel on game day for the first time," Scranton said.

"Excuse me?" asked the doctor.

"The tunnel that leads to the field. The first time you come out, and you see 100,000 fans going crazy, it's overwhelming. You can't help but stop and stare like you're a country bumpkin in the city for the first time."

"Ah, I understand," Daugava said. "But that player, he gets used to it, right?"

"Sort of," said Scranton, gently pushing a sheaf of papers across a glass coffee table. "Maybe I will, too."

After checking minor amendments that they agreed to in their last meeting, Doc signed the papers. Then he handed the pen to Riga, merely pointed at several dotted lines, and the big man signed his name without saying a word.

"Now what?" asked Scranton.

"Now," Doc said, "now you win."

CHAPTER 5

Catharine Payton Andrews / The American / Cleveland:

> *"As the sun warmed players in their unstained uniforms, none tainted with grass or dirt or blood yet, a football team posed for pictures, chatted with reporters and laughed with each other. Their bodies are machines that haven't been started, shiny and new. It is just a matter of time—six weeks, exactly—before the real grind would begin. The trench warfare, the hits, the blind sacks. Before the training room would become more familiar to them than their own home."*

So began Andrews' dispatch that afternoon, setting up her coverage. She filed from home, a far cry from the bustling newsrooms of the past. She had experienced a more staid environment when she came up as a reporter at a city daily, but most newsrooms were now extinct, or at the most, a shell of what existed years ago—engaging places with banter and jokes and bitterness and glib retorts. Now, all reporters worked from home, leaving only very small groups of editors to work in what resembled a small insurance office rather than a place with a constant, hurried buzz. She was too young to experience them; they were long gone by the time she was coming up in the business.

While newsrooms changed, so did sports. Andrews' love for the games and the action and the athletes took root early. Her father took her to games, explaining the intricacies of everything from a suicide squeeze on a baseball diamond to the safety blitz in football. Her middle name was an homage to his favorite football player, Walter Payton, who graced Soldier Field with his unorthodox style of running. She watched video of him with her dad, becoming amazed at the man in the navy blue and white jersey who seemed so much stronger than anyone on the field. He shoved defenders out of the way as he gracefully darted downfield.

"Why does he carry the ball like that?" she once asked, leaning back in her father's arms as the two watched the running back grip the ball with an outstretched hand on the television screen. "Didn't you tell me you shouldn't do that, that you have to tuck it in to protect it?"

Her dad smiled. "You should tuck it away, honey. But he was special. He could get away with it. Besides, look at him the second before he's tackled, watch what he does."

Catharine studied intently, then cried excitedly: "He tucks it away!" watching Payton protect the ball at the last second.

"Right," her dad said. "He protects it."

When she was 6, Catharine used to write "books," stories and sketches of dinosaurs and animals and storms. She would carefully fold and staple the pages. When she was 7 her dad signed her up for softball and she took to it immediately, her coordination and skills immediately ahead of almost every girl on the field.

When she was 11, her aunt came to visit, on a day when her team was playing to advance to the postseason. Catharine hit a sharp grounder to the third baseman, who stepped on the bag and ended the game in a force-out. She had run so hard all the way to first, she pulled a hamstring and, without looking back, knew her team had lost by the hollering and celebration going on. She limped back to the dugout, sat on the worn bench, and mindlessly rubbed her leg. For the first time after a game, Catharine cried.

Her aunt came into the dugout to take a picture of her. "Smile!" she had said cheerfully, and Catharine, at that moment, could not understand why anyone would say that after a loss. To her aunt she was an 11-year-old girl playing a game whose outcome would be forgotten over ice cream in a little while. But Catharine would never forget that feeling, the loss ending her season and the fact that some people, like her aunt, just didn't get it. She just wanted to win.

So it was a natural fit for Catharine, after high school and college, to become a sports writer. No matter what she did, she knew she would always be close to the games in one form or another.

Andrews' text prompt popped up on her screen almost as soon as she zapped the dispatch to her editor in New York. It was the final roster of players from the Stormcats public-relations department. Teams sent rosters and other news electronically, and the media guides—a reporter's bible—would be ready soon. They held every imaginable fact about a team, from statistics to bios on the players to the history of the team and league.

Andrews scanned the roster and checked the notes. Nothing new. She almost missed the only added entry, and would have if she were looking under names only. But Andrews was amazed at how big linemen were becoming. These days offensive linemen routinely were topping 320—a lot of weight to carry in their post-football days, she thought.

But when it came to the lines, a team hoped for an unmovable force on the offensive side, while having only slightly smaller but faster players on the defensive side.

The part that stopped her was "435."

99. Rotinom, Riga. DL 7-4, 435. None R

Riga Rotinom? Who was that? Seven-four, 435 pounds? Got to be a typo, Andrews thought. "None" indicated no college, which was rare these days. He hadn't played college or factory ball? Andrews was surprised; the name didn't register. The only thing that didn't surprise her was the "R" designate—a rookie, which made her feel somewhat better, that she hadn't missed this guy toiling somewhere in the league.

Worth a call, she thought.

CHAPTER 6

The offices at Emerald Lake Stadium became smaller as you walked down the main hall on the top floor. Scranton's office was a spacious work environment, with the couches, desk and occasional piece of artwork, all ringing a massive Persian rug that made guests dizzy if they looked down too long. Further down was the public-relations office. It was almost as large, but had files crammed along two sides and a couple of chairs wedged in. Steve Sails, the vice president of public relations, mindlessly scrolled the roster that a member of his staff furiously pecked out to members of the media and other interested parties.

He pushed on his glasses when his phone rang.

"Sails," he answered.

"Steve, this is Catharine Andrews of The American—just a quick question to start the year off right."

Sails smiled. "The year started off this morning with that giant bright yellow ball of light in the sky, don't you think Miss Andrews? They call it the sun. I mean, I almost forgot what snow was."

"Oh, c'mon, Steve, this is Cleveland. You can never forget what snow is."

He laughed. He loved banter, figuring it put reporters at ease. Andrews played along. It didn't cost anything to be friendly, and she was still going to ask whatever question she had anyway. Sometimes it was innocuous, like now, calling to check on something. Other times it was more serious. One time she had called Sails, who started his usual banter with "Hey have you seen that new movi—" only to be cut off with a run-on rapid-fire stream of questions: "No this is Andrews of The American can you tell me about three players being held in city jail since late last night?" Andrews knew a grand total of one city cop, and he happened to be on duty when the players were brought in on assault charges. He wasn't going to make a big deal of it, but when one of the players mouthed off to him he tipped her off. Today, though, conversation was a bit more carefree.

"What can I do for you?"

"I'm checking on this 'Rotinom' on the roster—is all this correct? Seven-four, 435?"

"Oh yeah, that's right. Hate to get hit by him, huh?" he chuckled. Sails was always chuckling.

Andrews—all 5-foot-4 of her—couldn't imagine.

"No, I—where did he come from? This guy wasn't on any prelim rosters," she said. "What's the deal?"

"Catharine, our scouts have scoured the world, and through their eyes and evaluations we find talented…"

The machine called "spin" was churning slowly, speeding up. At this rate, by the time the first preseason game started Sails would be in fine form.

"Steve, seriously, you don't materialize a seven-four guy—where's he from?"

Sails: "Actually, of all places, Riga."

Andrews: "As in Latvia? You have scouts in Latvia?"

"Catharine, we have one of the most extensive scouting systems in—"

"Steve," Andrews sighed, "what is the deal on this guy?"

Sails told her to hold, and searched his laptop for the player files. He pulled Rotinom's and took on a bit more serious tone. "He's from Riga, Latvia. His uncle brought him here a year ago."

"How old is he? Where did he play?"

Sails was quiet a second as he searched the player's bio. "20 years old…no college."

"Steve, you're telling me a professional football team is taking a flier on a guy who didn't play college football?" Andrews said, a mix of incredulity with a hint of sarcasm.

"Yeah," Sails admitted. "But like I said, we have scouts all over—"

"How does a guy in Latvia learn football—American football, not the kind most kids over there play?"

"Don't know, Catharine. Honestly, the guy is a recent find. I have to admit I don't know a whole lot about him, except I would want him on my side in a bar fight."

Andrews grunted. "No kidding—you and me both. Who's the scout?"

Sails paused again. "None listed."

Andrews sighed again. Non-answers—true or false—tended to test her patience.

"Steve, anything more on this guy that pops up, I'd like to know please. And I would like an interview. He didn't dress at Media Day, and for that matter he didn't exist, either, until I saw him on the roster."

"Hey, you know my policy—first to inquire, first to get called back."

"Many thanks. Have a good one," she said, and hung up.

Andrews walked to the standing globe in her study and spun it until she hit the Baltic Sea. There, sandwiched between Estonia and Lithuania, was the Latvian port city.

"How does a guy not play football, move 4,000 miles across the globe, and land in Cleveland to play professional football?" Andrews asked herself.

PART II

PRESEASON

CHAPTER 7

Camp Gantriel—never Campy, Camper or Campa-roo, always Camp—sat on a tall stool on the 50-yard line, watching his coaches watch the players, broken into units on another unseasonably warm day. Gantriel was a throwback—an all-business chieftain who concentrated on football and only football—from a perfectionist's point of view. He wore coaches' shorts and a golf shirt for practice, to be replaced on game days by a sports coat, coaches pants, sweater and knit hat that looked good only on him. He won reviews as a well-dressed coach, but it was his wife who chose his outfit, and it didn't matter. A reporter from a magazine once called to ask about his attire. He snapped: "This is a football team, not a fashion show," and promptly hung up. To the stoic Gantriel, time was everything. And he didn't have time for stupid questions.

Gantriel had been a 22-year-old graduate assistant at a tiny college in Indiana when the head coach died a week before the season began. Gantriel was promoted over a veteran coach who quit when he heard he wasn't going to be allowed to hire anyone. The school trustees figured they would save a few bucks and limp through a rebuilding season. But just because they weren't going to take the season seriously didn't mean Gantriel wouldn't. He made his squad believe in themselves, implemented his own brand of play-calling, and took them to the second round of the playoffs. The trustees couldn't overlook the job he had done, and he was offered a four-year deal. When he turned it down for a one-year deal, the surprised trustees quickly agreed, assuming if he stumbled they could can him and be off the hook from paying him.

What they didn't count on was Gantriel staying successful.

He created a small dynasty in a part of the country more known for its high school basketball than its college football. He hired assistants he could trust, put them on the road to aggressively recruit the kind of players he wanted to fit his playbook, and he won. So Gantriel continued signing one-year deals, and he continued getting a raise every year.

After 20 years, seeking that mid-life challenge, he joined the pro ranks as an assistant in Cleveland. Days after being hired, the head coach was fired after one too many sideline tantrums were caught on camera—this one against one of his own players. He apologized, but the tantrums lived online in perpetuity. Gantriel was promoted and led the team to two wins in its final three games. Cleveland won a total of five games that season, and the job was his.

Scranton may have suspected something in the coach, that leadership quality rarely seen but coveted from a front-office perspective. Or maybe it was just a hope that the new pro coach once again would sign only one-year deals. Either way, Gantriel stayed, built a winner, and became a fixture with Stormcats football.

But Camp Gantriel had endured a stretch of eight seasons with only two playoff appearances. Scranton always promised, publicly and privately, he would never fire a coach mid-season because of a won-loss record that favored the "L"s, and he stuck to his word. But this season's outcome was going to be the deal-breaker. So Gantriel sat and watched from his coaches' stool—used in part for vantage, and so his assistants always knew where he was.

Gantriel's wife once told him football practice is to a game what gardening is to a flower. As a gardener must plan, dig, seed, nurture and protect the plant, so must a football team work on its preparations. It takes months of hard work, repetitive drills, conditioning and scouting the opponent to get a team ready for its season. When the seeding is done, a rose blooms. When its seeding is done, a football team is ready for its opponent.

Gantriel scanned the field. Pockets of running backs took pitchouts over and over. Quarterbacks not dishing the ball to the backs were placed in units that met defenses the Stormcats could expect to face. And defensive players lined up to react against various running and passing plays. But the one player who drew Gantriel's attention was the tallest one on the field.

He saw Rotinom bat down balls from his middle-linebacker position. He watched as he reacted instantaneously to run plays up the middle. If a running back were fortunate enough to get through the defensive line, all Rotinom would need was a hand on his jersey, and he would seamlessly reel him in. In 12 passing plays, Rotinom batted four balls. In 12 running plays, he made six tackles. Not one offensive lineman could stop Rotinom from moving to either side to stop end-around plays. His reaction time slowed only when the ball was thrown deep, way past him. And frankly, those plays were rarely his responsibility.

In all his years of coaching, Gantriel had not seen a defensive player like Rotinom. And the guy had materialized almost out of the proverbial thin air.

Gantriel recalled the day Scranton had called him in at the end of Media Day and told him he wanted the coach to look at a player who could be a "project." It was Gantriel's call on the guy; all Scranton asked was an evaluation. Gantriel didn't have a problem. The two got along well, knowing the key to their relationship was letting the other do his job. Privately, Gantriel highly doubted the player would turn out to be anything but fodder in practice, a kid who would be overrun and outclassed by more experienced players.

By lunchtime on the first day of practice, Camp Gantriel knew he was wrong.

When the team broke from agility and speed drills, several offensive players huddled by the portable water coolers. With all the technology that had come along, one thing that was not replaced were the old-fashioned coolers of water and sports drinks. Of course, nutritionists now were able to measure exactly how much liquid each man would need, and some players followed their "PHGs"—personal hydration guidelines—closely. Others did it the old-fashioned way: They drank when they were thirsty.

The players, drenched in sweat early during the twice-daily workouts, breathed deep, swirling water in their mouths and dumping cupfuls over their heads. There was no breeze to offer even the slightest relief on the late July day.

"That big guy—99—dang he's strong," Culpepper huffed between drills. "It's like all he did was touch me, threw me off. Next thing I know I'm down."

"I can't reach that guy to block, can't get close to him,"

said McAdams, bending over at the waist—a sign of being tired, and a gesture Gantriel despised.

"Carver, you all right man?" asked Bronx Thomas, eyeing his backfield partner, who sat silently on a bench.

"He got dinged," Culpepper said between gulps, "on the off-tackle run. No one picked up the big guy and he slammed him."

Carver took a sip of water to clear the cobwebs. "He's like a brick wall with legs, man. Guy's got speed to go with that size."

"Who the hell is he?" asked McAdams.

"Don't know," Thomas replied. "Just want the season to start, man, so he can hit someone with another jersey."

A whistle blew them into final drills, as they crushed the cups and trudged back for more.

Gantriel motioned for his assistant head coach to run the drills, then called over Cy Francis, the defensive coordinator.

"Coach," Francis said, as he trotted over to Gantriel's stool near the sidelines.

"What do you make of 99?" Gantriel asked.

"I don't know where this guy came from, but he's got it," Francis said.

"You know all I know," Gantriel said. "Tell me about his moves."

"Never seen anything like it. Guy goes to the flat like no one. And his strength is amazing. Don't know what they're feeding him over there in Latvia or Estonia or wherever he's from, but he's been eatin' his Wheaties, 'cause—"

"What about the plays?" Gantriel cut him off. "Is he reaching out to grab the runner because he was out of position? How's he reacting?"

"Coach, it's like he memorized the whole playbook. He's moving where he needs to be every time."

Gantriel looked at his assistant for a second, then turned his attention to the field. The biggest, fastest and strongest athletes in professional sports were in the NPL. Most had been playing football since they were 6 or 7. They were stars every step of the way. Few players made it to college on full rides, fewer to the factories. The odds of being able to grace a professional stadium's field were more than long. A dream was the closest many would get to playing here. Yet here was a guy who had been in this country supposedly for less than a year and he looked like he had it all.

Practice went on, the drills were run over and over, until Gantriel signaled the horn for final laps. He'd have to talk with 99 some time. But he had to give Scranton credit. Wherever he dug up this kid, he looked like the real thing.

CHAPTER 8

The locker room underwent its usual transformation from pristine, modern-looking dressing room to a 12-year-old's bedroom in seconds flat. Jerseys were stripped off and tossed in the vicinity of laundry bins, but usually not in them. Pads were pulled out, tape was cut off and left strewn on the floor. Steam wafted from showers as players milled about, some with towels draped, some wearing shorts, some naked. It was a collection of large bodies, most of whom had two immediate goals to accomplish: Get clean, then get fed.

Tiger Canton glanced at the schedules posted for weight-room times before sitting on a bench next to Rotinom. The big man had said few if any words to anyone on the field, but he always listened intently to coaches.

"Hey, 99—where'd you play college ball?" asked Canton, a third-year-linebacker.

"Didn't play."

Canton looked dumbly. "Where'd you learn the moves man?"

"Studied."

"You studied football—you never played in college? What position did you play in high school?"

Rotinom stared blankly for a second, then said: "Never played. No football in high school."

Canton pulled on his socks and stopped for a minute. "How did you study? What, you read books?"

"Read, saw TV, watched videos, played pretend."

"Pretend?"

"I would go to a park and envision players around me, making the moves I saw them make on television," Rotinom said in a very slight Eastern European accent. "I would run in the direction of the ball carrier."

Canton stared and then shook his head. "Unreal, dude. I've never seen anything like it. Hey you wanna go grab a—"

"Have to go, man," Rotinom said, pulling on a golf shirt.

Canton watched as Rotinom picked up a gym bag and left.

The general mood in the locker room was relaxed, though tired. The only hurried pace came from the club-house boys, who were gathering up the clothes for the high-speed washers. The washers had been marketed about the same time a company had changed the formula for detergent, and washing and drying took mere minutes, rather than an hour or more. Only one more round of cuts were coming, and because of injuries suffered to a backup center, a long shot free-agent running back and two low draft picks, it was almost a foregone conclusion who would make the team. Only a few more days of training camp and training table for meals, along with life in the dorm, and then it would be back to normal routines—homes, wives, girlfriends, going out, and no calls for lights out.

The players came out of the lockers in small groups at a time and made their way to the dining room. Scranton had insisted on training tables and dorms during preseason to foster camaraderie. It was an old-fashioned tradition, and Gantriel had stuck with it. Within minutes, coaches and players were lining up at the buffet of grilled bone-less chicken, roasted vegetables, baked potatoes, salad and pudding. Food choices hadn't changed much over the years, but preparation had. New ovens roasted food faster, "power-healthy" herbs were mixed in with the vegetables, and dietitians cut the amount of sugar in recipes for pudding, putting in vitamin supplements.

It was about halfway through the meal when Gantriel looked around and didn't see the behemoth anywhere. He scanned the room. No Rotinom. The other coaches ate with as much gusto as the players. Just then the players' tones hushed as they saw Brooks Scranton make a rare appearance through a side door. He approached the coaches' table, where he whispered something to Gantriel. The two got up and walked outside.

"Coach," Scranton said, "I just received a call. The new player I told you about, Riga Rotinom, had to leave."

"Leave?" Gantriel said. "What happened?"

"Apparently his uncle, his guardian, had an emergency in the family and had to take him back to Latvia. Said they would be back in two weeks."

"Two weeks," was all Gantriel could say. "I haven't even talked to this kid, Brooks. I saw him on the field for a few hours today, that's it. We'll be almost done with exhibition games by then."

"Coach," Scranton started off again, "what did you think of him? In the mix with other players, considering he has no formal training?"

"Amazing," Gantriel said. "Freak of nature. Don't know where you found him but he's got the goods. He spends time with coaches and films and…" Gantriel let his voice trail, shaking his head thinking what Rotinom could become.

"Well coach, you could save a roster spot for him," Scranton said. "Excused absence. Family emergency."

Gantriel stopped. Rotinom was too good to be true. Despite what the coach had seen, saving a roster spot would mean cutting someone and gambling the kid returns, safely, and is willing to learn. He didn't even know his personality.

"There's no attitude or skeletons on this kid, no criminal record I don't know about?" Gantriel said.

"None, coach. Clean bill of health. Our medical folks cleared him. Our detectives dug deep—clean. Just raw talent in a kid who wasn't in the position to play the game because of where he grew up."

Gantriel thought for a moment, but his thoughts weren't clear. All he could see was Rotinom's outstretched arms batting balls that no other defensive player in the league could have reached. The slight thrill in his gut battled the cautious feeling that usually came to him when he made big decisions. If they held a roster position he would have two weeks before the opener against Kansas City.

"OK, sir, we'll save a spot."

CHAPTER 9

The days continued, as did the summer heat, with the only relief coming in the steady breeze off Lake Erie. Players practiced, running their repetitive drills under the sun and the watchful eyes of Gantriel and his coaches. Scranton told Gantriel the only contact he had had with the doctor was a phone call, saying he and Rotinom would be back soon. Gantriel was not one to worry about what he could not control, so he wasn't overly concerned.

Catharine continued writing medical-sports stories for The American and talking with players. Gantriel liked to close practices, meaning the media couldn't watch. He didn't want to leak new plays in the works. No need to give anyone an edge in a game when every little advantage counted.

The Stormcats started preseason, a wary time for Gantriel. Preseason was a time for players to take game hits, so their bodies remember what it's like, and for coaches to watch how players react in game conditions. It was an opportunity for second- and third-stringers to show they could perform and be ready should a starter go down. Gantriel was set on the four quarterbacks the team would carry, and most of the units were in place. The league had decided years earlier to expand rosters and allow teams to carry a quartet of QBs, and it worked out fine. They didn't have to scramble to sign someone when a player went down with an injury.

It was just a matter of time before the opener in late August. The players continued holing up in the dorm that was part of the Emerald Lake Stadium campus. Some teams still went offsite for training camp, but when the stadium was built, it incorporated dining halls and dorms and other top-of-the-line facilities, including what amounted to a small hospital. The only thing that didn't change was the team's insistence that players remain together. It was supposed to lead to camaraderie. Of course, the whole process had to be incorporated into the standard player's contract.

"Lights out" came at 10 p.m. when a coach or team manager would make the announcement via digital intercom to the rooms. Of course, players would ignore it, until their bodies wound down for sleep.

Some played video games. Others read. A few held bull sessions, those late-night talks about everything and nothing. Rarely did they talk about football.

Jon LeBon, a wide receiver, Pun Wisgenti, Dunwoody Culpepper and Brock McAdams sat up one night before the lights-out call in Bronx Thomas' and Reilly Carver's room.

"I'm just saying, if you had a five-pound weight fall on your hand, would you cry?" Carver asked McAdams.

"No, man, I ain't gonna cry."

"Ten—what about a ten-pound weight—would you cry then?"

"I told you—I ain't crying."

LeBon joined in. "What if it had a nail sticking out from it, and it went through your hand? Would you cry then?"

McAdams remained firm. "No way, man. I can take

that fullback from Green Bay coming at me, I can take that."

Wisgenti said, "What if your dog—your trusty hunting dog—had a ten-pound weight with spikes dropped on it, and he died right in front of you?"

McAdams said, "I wouldn't cry; I would want to get even with the guy who did it."

"But what if it fell off a shelf, it was an accident?" Wisgenti said.

McAdams thought for a minute. "Yeah, I might cry then, maybe."

"Well, that settles it, then," Carver said.

"What?" McAdams asked.

"You're a big baby."

McAdams grabbed a football and threw it in the general direction of Carver as everyone laughed at the gag. Everyone but McAdams knew where the conversation had been heading. McAdams, a beefy crew-cutted lineman who walked like both knees were going to cave in at any minute, simply laid back in his chair.

Culpepper: "Hey Frenchy, they got French fries over there in France?"

LeBon: "How the hell do I know? I've never been there. But I'll tell you something."

"What?" Culpepper asked.

"If I went over there, and I went to a McDonald's, and they didn't have French fries, and I was really, really hungry, man, I have to say…" his voice trailed off.

"What?" Culpepper asked again, the others listening.

"Well, then," as he glanced at McAdams, "I think then that I would cry."

Everyone laughed as McAdams leaned back again and said, "Aw, man…"

Just then the intercom buzzed with coach Francis' voice and his familiar refrain that began to sound like lyrics to a song: "Lights out, lights out. Get 'em out, lights out. Hit the hay."

"Man, Francis gotta be happy these days," said Culpepper.

"Why's that?" asked LeBon.

"Cause he's got the big guy coming back. You remember—99, the one-hit wonder from a couple weeks ago?"

McAdams groaned. Carver winced.

"Yeah, what happened to that guy?" Thomas wondered. "There one day, then gone."

"Some sort of excused absence," Wisgenti said.

"That guy was a freakin' skyscraper," said McAdams.

"But he comes back, and Francis is gonna be one happy dog," Culpepper said.

Everyone nodded.

"Gonna be a hot one tomorrow," Thomas said, remembering the heat the day they saw Rotinom on the field.

"June, July, August—90 degrees and warm. There's your summary weather," Wisgenti said.

Some nodded, but no one chuckled. Few ever got Wisgenti's puns.

The players headed to their respective rooms.

CHAPTER 10

Rotinom returned as quietly as he had left. He showed up in Gantriel's office early on the Tuesday after the third and final preseason game. Gantriel acted like a parent who's happy to see his teenager safe, yet angry that he came home after curfew.

It was a short conversation.

"Here 99, study this. Learn everything in this," Gantriel said, thrusting the playbook at him, its inside cover labeled with threats of fines if the book were lost. Gantriel never sent the playbook electronically. He still believed in the hard-copy book. Years ago players used to keep them in the trunks of their cars, out of sight.

"Yes, Coach," was all Rotinom said as he filled Gantriel's office doorway.

So far, other than Andrews' initial inquiry, no one had asked about Rotinom. Out of sight, out of mind. Andrews had her plate full with medical research and keeping tabs on the injured Stormcats from preseason, though no one was out of commission. The real frenzy—the regular season— would begin soon. Sails had gotten back to her with scant knowledge of Rotinom. The big man was still an unknown commodity.

Gantriel stuck to his plan and shuttled four quarterbacks in and out, getting them used to in-game conditions as much as possible. As much as he liked to win, preseason was more for conditioning, preparing and evaluating than winning. So veteran John Balany, loner Joey Bexar, perennial backup Wayne Tarrant and a young Cuya Aconttie each took snaps, threw downfield and worked on the two-minute offense, that final surge that required leadership as well as stamina.

Of the quartet, Aconttie was the longest of long shots to make the team, but he did. He grew up south of Cleveland, and as such was like a college basketball team's walk-on from the hometown, drawing cheers when he had a rare chance to enter a game with a lead. Aconttie could move and zip around the field, but he was barely six feet, and that had thrown off teams considering drafting him.

Rotinom was the first in the locker room after the final preseason game, getting taped and dressed and ready to hit the practice field.

"Where you been Latvia?" asked LeBon, the fastest player on the team. Some of the players had taken to calling Rotinom by his home country.

"Latvia," replied Rotinom, who stood, his seven-foot-four frame slowly reaching up in the locker room, a building rising of sorts, and left for the field before any more small talk could be made.

"Well, that answers that," said Wisgenti, nearby.

"Talkative guy, ain't he?" McAdams said to the receivers.

The Cleveland practices for the week had a primary goal: Stop Kansas City's run game. The units were broken down and teams lined up against their scout-team counterparts, who wore stretched-out orange caps atop their helmets and acted as opposing offenses and defenses.

The defensive unit was expected to position itself based on how "Kansas City" lined up. The first two plays were off-tackle runs; Rotinom made both stops, the first after 4 yards, the second after 2. On the third play Rotinom shot to his left almost as soon as the ball was snapped and batted down a pass to the flat. Outcome: 6 yards, expected punt.

"Nice stop big guy."

"Ninety-nine, way to be."

"Way to plug it up guy."

It might have been an anomaly, or maybe it was the slowness of the scout team, but the next series of plays ended pretty much the same way. And the one after that. Gantriel celebrated by replacing Rotinom with another linebacker.

OK, Gantriel thought, I think the defense is ready. All one of them.

Play continued, and Gantriel called an early and merciful end to practice in the August heat. But preparation would continue in the theater.

The theater is what Gantriel called the film room, another top-of-the-line facility for the Stormcats to break down film of the opposition. Even though it actually was digital recordings, it was still called "film," an homage to the sport's early days. The technology they used allowed for no blurry movement or shaking when Gantriel hit a pause or rewind button in the middle of a play, to show where someone was or, as often was the case, wasn't supposed to be.

The team filed in and Gantriel put the hand-held remote clicker to use the way some people absent-mindedly click a ball-point pen continuously.

"You see here? Their line is shifting to the strong side— they make it look like the play is going that way. But the quarterback stops, waits just a second, and throws quickly to the weak side. That's designed. Now watch the blockers help—Mr. Canton, you do know your weak side from your strong side?"

Gantriel had signaled a slightly sleepy looking Tiger Canton who, despite the fact that uncomfortable chairs were purposefully used to keep players awake, had nearly dozed off.

"Yes sir, coach."

"Good, Mr. Canton, I wouldn't want you to miss out on anything."

Players snickered. Gantriel managed to always catch someone nodding off. Canton, though, wasn't nodding off. He watched as if he were a kid watching his favorite movie for the 10th time, listening and taking it all in. He loved football, and wouldn't have wanted to be anywhere else. He sat, he watched, and he studied as he mindlessly felt the railroad-like indented scar across his right knee. Gantriel glanced at the back of the room before starting again, seeing Rotinom stare intently, his eyes darting at the screen, also taking it all in.

Outside, Andrews waited for players to head to their cars, hoping to catch a couple for quick interviews. She leaned against her car, scribbling key words of things she wanted to ask several of the players.

Then the doors swung open, and players laughed and hoisted gym bags over their shoulders. Some had wives or girlfriends waiting to pick them up, but most had left cars in the lot. Several had self-driving units—SDUs, they were called.

Suddenly, she saw the big guy—her internal reference for Rotinom—veer to the side of the lot. She had no idea how dominating he was in practice, because practices were closed. Because of his "excused absence," as Sails had told her, she hadn't seen him in games. But she hadn't forgotten about his roster line: Seven-four, 435. She lurched away, clutching her PDR and notebook and walking fast toward Rotinom, who was walking with a small, conservatively dressed man. The man saw Andrews out of the corner of his eye, whispered something briefly to Rotinom, and turned. But Rotinom kept going to the car.

"May I help you, Miss…"

"Andrews," Andrews said. "I'm with The American. I'd like to speak to Riga Rotinom for a minute."

"I'm afraid we have to go," Daugava said.

"I'm Catharine Andrews from The American," Andrews said, quickly repeating herself to let the man know he was talking to a reporter. That always had to be out there immediately so there were no false pretenses. "Who are you?"

"My name is Dr. Daugava, Janis Daugava," he said gently.

"Well, nice to meet you, but I would like to speak with Riga—"

"I am afraid that is not possible, Miss," he said politely.

Politeness didn't help. Andrews had little patience for someone preventing an interview she wanted, especially when the person had no business doing so.

"Sir, I just need—who are you?" she suddenly demanded.

"I am Riga's uncle," the man said in his quiet and patient tone. "And I am sorry, but we have to leave. Some other time, I am afraid."

With that he put his hat back on and turned toward the car. Running after him wasn't going to help now. But Andrews had seen for herself—the big guy was back.

She caught up with some of the other players, getting

some quotes before heading home, happy with her tiny nugget of information: The big guy was spotted. He's on the team. Now all she had to do was see him in action and talk to him.

CHAPTER 11

The small sports car shook as it zigzagged through city streets, a jazzy beat from the speakers drowning out the noise of the engine. Its driver grunted slightly when it turned sharply—first left, then a quick right, then back left. The compact sports car raced around a pole, fish-tailing slightly. The driver accelerated and nicked a garbage pail, sending it flying high, its cover spinning dramatically and its contents scattering in midair. Just then, seconds before seeing a "Leaving city limits / Have a nice day!" sign, he hit a main avenue and sped up. The car ventured up a hill with a dropoff, soared for three seconds, and came down smoothly. VOOM! The driver pushed a button to supercharge the engine, and now he was really off, snow-capped mountains in the distance. He swerved around a slow-poking sedan, then straddled the middle of the two-lane highway. Then, without warning, the car stopped.

Game Over.

"Aw," said McAdams. "I was almost there, I could see the mountains."

"Nice going Brock man," said Thomas, who had watched the lineman take most of the turns on the video-racing game with a deft touch. "But now watch a pro. Call the Indy 500; I'm going on the circuit!"

Teammates laughed as McAdams grunted and took off his virtual-reality goggles. Thomas swiped his game card across the machine's sensors, donned the goggles, sat in the plush seat and put his hand on the gearshift. The jazzy background music started as the game read his card and scrolled "Welcome, Mr. Thomas!" before flashing "3-2-1-GO!" The fullback shifted and he was off, in his own world for the next 120 seconds, maybe more if he could get to the mountain stage.

It was the closest way Thomas and McAdams could get to racing; their contracts included strict clauses about off-field activity restrictions. Getting injured in something as mundane as a pickup basketball game could void their contracts, and as fair as owner Brooks Scranton had been, he let every player know he would hold them to their contracts. Racing cars was out. So were hang-gliding, bungee-jumping, snowboarding and other action sports. It was a key reason why many of the players got good at playing pool.

The players were at ajo, an upscale restaurant-bar-arcade downtown, frequented by many of the Stormcats. The trio of siblings who owned the restaurant liked having the players in and treated them more like customers than celebrities, not bugging them for autographs. The players liked ajo because they could unwind and often were given private tables in the back where patrons wouldn't disturb them. Besides, at ajo, the steaks were huge and the beer was cold. It was a place to unwind, a playground for grown-ups.

Owners Olivia and Julia Simpson surveyed their patrons and wait staff. Their brother Adam was holed up in a back-room office as usual, going over the books. Olivia was the muscle who hired (and fired) the staff, and Julia was the hostess who coordinated reservations. Olivia had a slight smile on her face. A Tuesday night and the place was already filling. Ajo was turning into one of the hot spots downtown.

Carver, Thomas, McAdams, Wisgenti, LeBon, Culpepper and Balany—a usual group of offensive players—found themselves at ajo frequently during the season. They always found one reason or another to celebrate—a win, a birthday, something. Conversation always bounced from topic to topic.

"Wallow," said Carver.

"What?" one of the players asked at the round table in the back, curved paneling forming a shelter around them, framed sports magazine covers from the past lining the wall.

"Wallow," he repeated. "It's a good word. "So's 'Chunnel.' "

"What's a 'Chunnel?' " asked McAdams.

"It's the tunnel underneath the English Channel between England and France," Wisgenti said.

"Why do they call it a 'Chunnel?' " McAdams asked again.

All resisted a smart response.

"Channel, tunnel—put them together," said Carver.

"Oh," was all McAdams said, eager to change the subject.

"Big ol' tunnel," Culpepper said. "Almost as big as that 99."

"He keeps being that one-man defense out there, and that's fine by me," LeBon said to Wisgenti. "Pin 'em in their own zone and let's go score."

"I hear you," Balany piped in. "Let's go score."

"Score!" shouted McAdams.

Just then a waitress arrived with a tray full of salads. The organically grown greens arrived under mounds of crumbled bleu cheese.

"You always get salads every time you score?" Wisgenti quizzed McAdams. The big lineman grunted as he reached for the pepper.

"Yeah, he's gonna spike the lettuce," said Culpepper.

Balany changed the subject and turned to Carver and Thomas, his backfield mates.

"You get the additional plays down? You study?"

Both nodded. Gantriel had added several plays late in preseason, trying to take advantage of Carver's throwing ability. Flea flickers weren't used that often but when they worked, it was a sight. Gantriel's plays were precise instructions that he expected everyone to follow, and that meant muscle memory: Run them, run them, run them, and then run them some more.

"Only thing I'm studying tonight is this steak that's comin', " McAdams said as he pushed the salad plate away to make room for the porterhouse and slab of crisp onions. McAdams loved food as much as football, and ajo had one of the newer grills, where you could order your steak by specific temperature instead of the old-fashioned "medium" or "medium rare."

"Speaking of steak, anyone want to go hunting this year?" asked Culpepper in his drawl. "We get a week off, head down to Jawjah, hit the woods."

"What do 'steak' and 'hunting' have to do with each other?" asked McAdams.

Players stared.

"Kidding," McAdams said.

Thomas shook his head no. "I'll stick to eating; you can go hunt. Call me for the barbecue." Carver nodded in agreement.

"Aww, ya'll don't know what you're missing."

Steaks arrived, and the waitress passed them out like she was dealing a deck of cards.

"Jenny, you hunt?" Culpepper asked.

"No," she said, putting a plate down. "I eat."

Thomas: "That's what I'm talking about!"

"Nothing beats a good burger on the grill," the waitress said, finishing the food distribution. "Anyone need anything?" A chorus of "No, thanks" was mumbled so she turned and left.

"Best burger I ever had was at this little place in Toledo," Balany said as his teammates started cutting into their beef, almost simultaneously. "Spent a weekend there once when I was in college. This little mom-and-pop place, they made it exactly how you wanted. Cooked to perfection. Morning I'm leaving, I stop at the drive-through, figure I'll get myself one more of these burgers. I swipe my card as I drive around to the pickup window. Guy hands me a bag, and it's heavy. He handed me fries along with the burger, and I didn't order them. When I look back he's handing me two more bags, and they're both real heavy."

His teammates chewed as they listened to his story.

"So I peek in one of the bags, and it's got about six burgers in it. Now I figure I got about a dozen of these burgers, and the guy looks at me and says 'Have a nice day!' So I start to pull out with all this food, and I get a few feet away when I hear the guy yelling 'Hey! hey! hey!' I figure he realizes his mistake. So I peer out the window, and the guy is holding a cup out the drive-through window and he says, 'You forgot your shake!' "

The players all laughed. Wisgenti bellowed before asking "So what'd you do?"

"Gave it back. Good angel appeared on my shoulder, and spoke louder than the bad angel. Besides, I liked the burgers, but what am I gonna do with a dozen burgers?"

"I'd have chowed 'em," McAdams said.

Meanwhile, on another side of town, in a quiet eatery nestled between a drugstore and some apartments, Doc Daugava sat, finishing a grilled-cheese sandwich and bowl of tomato soup. He ate quietly at the counter, his thoughts to himself. There were no games, no crowds here like at ajo. Just a few tables, a counter and waitresses in gingham dresses. Rotinom was back in the apartment, quietly reading the playbook. That's all Rotinom did. In the beginning, on the first day Doc picked up Rotinom from practice, he couldn't wait to get home, to make sure Riga was all right. He was anxious and wanted reassurance. That day, after they arrived home and Doc saw Rotinom was OK from any hits he took or tackles he made on his first real day as a football player against other players, Doc breathed a sigh of relief. Since then, he still made his daily checks with Rotinom, as any protective uncle would do. But he was OK, he was always OK. Doc and Riga had only each other.

And at home Andrews munched on chicken-fried rice and sipped iced tea. She ran the name "Rotinom" through a voters' registration data base. Nothing. Then she tried driver's licenses. Empty. Criminal records. Zip. She tried electronic phone books. Again, nothing.

"Guy's clean," she mumbled to her dog, Ginger, who was perched by her knee, waiting patiently for any bits of rice to fall. "Also nonexistent."

She scooped at the cardboard carry-out container with her chopsticks as tiny pieces of carrots and chicken clung to bits of egg. It was halfway to her mouth when she had another thought: Daugava. She had asked Sails about the guy after her encounter in the parking lot. All she knew was how to spell his name. She came up empty on the voter pool and other searches and went back to her rice. A text popped up from her editor, who was asking about a story she was working on regarding the Stormcats' injuries going into the first game of the year. Sidetracked momentarily, she had lost track of which databases she had searched for the player and doctor. She glanced around, trying to recall where she could still run a check. She saw her car keys laying by her purse, then realized she had forgotten Driver's licenses on the doctor. She typed in his name and came up with one hit:

Daugava, Janis

DOB: 4-4-64

504 60th St., Apt. 2, CLE

Ha! She had little, but it was something. He was 64 and lived in an apartment. OK, it wasn't much. Actually it was only slightly better than squat, but it was a start. She knew where to find him. Driver's licenses fell in and out of favor as a public record over the years, and she was glad they were open now. She found nothing on him in her company's archives; no one had done a story that even mentioned him. Sometimes those passing references shined a little light into who a fellow was. Years earlier he might have been photographed working somewhere, or making news someplace else. But nothing on Daugava.

"Ginger," she said to the mutt, whose tongue hung in anticipation of dropping food, "I am going to see a doctor tomorrow. How do you like that?"

Ginger responded by drooling.

PART III

THE SEASON

CHAPTER 12

Catharine Payton Andrews / The American / Cleveland:

"The three Stormcats who suffer from 'turf toe' said they would play Sunday against Kansas City. The injury usually occurs from playing on a harder, artificial surface. But the trio of linemen spent all of preseason on grass. That has at least one doctor questioning how this happened…

Andrews filed her latest "hurt log" to her editor Saturday afternoon, then left to try to find Daugava. But no one was home in the two-story building in an older part of Cleveland. So she attached a note to her business card and slid it in the mail slot with Daugava's name on it. Then it was back home to make calls on another story and wait for his call, which she suspected would not come. But she had to try.

Andrews saw the flecks of green and white as she drove through the hilly neighborhood on the way home. Giant banners hung from windows of stores, flags waved from their posts on the 1940s houses that lined the street. A few political signs were planted in yards, urging residents to vote for a school levy. Someone had altered "Vote for our schools" by scrawling "STORMCATS!" in place of schools. Andrews figured the artist probably smiled to himself at his "wit." Probably the brightest thing he did in a week, she thought.

The callback never came. Andrews prepared as much as she could for the season opener: Parking pass in hand, credentials ready, all electronics charged and ready. She took Ginger for a long walk through her neighborhood, squirrels scampering and Ginger tugging on her leash the whole way.

The Stormcats themselves were going through their final paces preparing for Kansas City. Gantriel had run them, drilled them, and run them some more. Anyone who had not memorized the playbook by now was going to be seriously lost on the field this weekend, when the game would make practice feel like slow motion.

Meanwhile, Cuya Aconttie spent time at his grandmother's. Rosalinda was a die-hard Stormcats fan even before her grandson put on the uniform. They sat at her small kitchen table in the old wood-framed house where she had lived her entire life. Aconttie knew every inch of it; growing up, he and his parents had checked in on her all the time. He had raked her leaves, cut her grass, carried boxes up from the basement. She would slip him a dollar or two as a reward. She was the best cook he knew, prompting him to tell friends she could make a glass of milk taste better just by pouring it.

"You remember that girl you brought by here once?" his grandmother asked.

"Which one nana?" he said, smiling because he knew the answer and the story.

"The one who asked me what was on television, and I told her the Stormcats. And she said—"

"She said, 'No, I mean what sport?' "

His grandmother laughed.

"You DO remember."

"She wasn't around long," Aconttie said.

"Sharp mind like that, I don't know why," his grandmother snickered.

The two talked and reminisced, with the only thing different being coffee, not chocolate milk, that Aconttie drank now.

"I'm proud of you Cuya," she said seriously. "You're going to make that team proud, too."

"Thanks nana," said Aconttie—respectfully aloud as he wondered how he would make anyone proud sitting on the bench.

The following morning, the town was buzzing. The hype was on for the opener, with constant video coverage locally and nationally. The national sports network that didn't broadcast the pay-per-view telecast was always interviewing someone or analyzing what could or would happen.

Brooks Scranton was his usual controlled self on the outside, but inside he could barely contain his nerves. He tried to put his deal with Daugava out of his mind but couldn't. He had followed all the deadlines with the league office, filing his rosters and injury reports. Sunday hadn't come fast enough.

Across town, in his small apartment he shared with Rotinom, Doc was as nervous. He felt so much pride in his nephew, who was about to be tested on a grand stage. No high school football, no college. Millions would watch when Cleveland and Kansas City played. Riga seemed— was—calm. Always. Doc felt confident and scared at the same time.

The game was a sell-out and had been for some time. A warm breeze blew through the stadium as summer tried to hang on. Gantriel was the first among the players and coaches to arrive. He didn't notice him at first, but Rotinom was there, mostly dressed and ready for stretches and pregame drills, even though they were hours away from taking the field. He kept to himself in a far corner of the locker room. In the time he had been with the team, a few players, like Canton, had approached him, and most gave up any attempts at conversation. Rotinom didn't come off as stand-offish, but his one-word answers bored them after a while. But the guy went hard in practice, and clearly looked to be an anchor on defense. Any lack of conversational skills were overlooked.

Reporters and front-office staff mingled in the various levels of the press box. Waitresses in Stormcat-colored skirts walked between them, offering to get coffee or soda for the reporters who were filing in, testing equipment and making sure everything was connected and charged. The new batteries that had been developed just a few years before, though, usually meant no one had to worry about any devices dying in the middle of the game.

It wasn't until the reporters actually pulled out the depth charts that the team issued on game day when they saw the listing for "99: Rotinom, Riga" among the middle linebackers. No one had seen him: He wasn't part of media day, practices remain closed, and he hadn't even been on the sidelines for preseason games. He was a complete mystery. When Andrews filed into her seat she looked around at the stadium. While she kept a stoic look on the outside, the kid inside her rattled around. She loved sports, and she loved being here on Sunday afternoons, seeing the players stretch and jump nervously in place as they readied for battle. She took it all in for a few minutes, then read the day's report from the team. The league required all injuries to be disclosed to create an even playing field, so to speak. Reporting injuries equally meant no team could sandbag another by keeping a key player out of the game, then suddenly springing him on the opponent. This way, everyone had an idea who would play, who could play, and who was doubtful.

She might have been the only reporter in press row who was not surprised when she saw Rotinom's entry atop the middle linebackers. There was something mysterious about the guy; she couldn't put her finger on it. He doesn't play in preseason, yet he's starting today. He didn't play college ball, yet someone found this guy. Lots of questions.

Players dressed in padded pants but no shoulder pads. They stretched and lined in formations to run plays they had worked on countless times. Andrews and her seatmate Dallas Trent watched. She lifted her gaze from the field to the crowd and then to the skyline as the players finished pregame routines and filed back to their respective lockers.

The stadium filled, as tail-gaters rolled in and found their seats. Camera crews were in place on the field. The warm, steamy aromas wafted from concession stands. A dad held his little boy's hand as they walked in the corridor, the father looking for their section while the small boy stared up in wonder at the pennants and people and colors and vendors. Peanut hawkers made their way to their allotted section, trudging their basket full of bags. Ice-cream vendors would have a heavier load, freezer boxes full of frozen ices, refreshing at the beginning part of the season but not a big seller toward the end.

"Ladies and gentlemen," a deep voice boomed. "Welcome to Emerald Lake Stadium, for the start of the 2028 season!" The crowd cheered as the scoreboard lit with players' bios, each one sponsored by a different company. "Now, if you would please rise and remove your caps…" A local television celebrity who had a nice voice was announced along with an honor guard, the crowd rose, and the anthem was sung.

The announcer continued, emphasizing certain words along the way: "Welcome to today's gaaaaame between the visiting Kansas City Explorers"—He paused to let the crowd unleash its immediate 'boooo'—"and yourrr Cleveland Stormcats!" The 90,000 fans shifted their boos into a roar welcoming the hometown team.

The huddled players had formed a tight mass, jumping in place, shaking their legs—anything to stay loose until they received the signal from the staffer working the tunnel entrance. When he heard "Stormcats" he was on. He turned to the team, making sure he was out of the way, and yelled "Go go go!" The players rushed, their mass of energy unleashed through the cheerleaders' pom-pom aisle, along the end zone, spilling up the sidelines to their benches.

The players watched as ceremonies continued. A former player who looked to be 100 was led to the center of the field, along with a host of dignitaries and officials.

Balany and Canton, the captains, made their way to the coaches, then walked to the center of the field for the coin toss.

"I thought he was dead?" mused Culpepper on the sidelines.

"He is. They thaw him out for the big games," Wisgenti said dryly.

"Your guys gonna take care of business?" Balany asked Canton with a slight smile as the two walked to midfield.

"You know it, just put the ball in the end zone, and we'll keep 'em out," replied Canton.

Balany loved this walk. He had done it for years, and it never got old. He was in his 30s, and he took less and less for granted—games, teammates, even the simple walk for the coin toss. His body was mostly free of the scar lines that so many of his teammates had, and he had stayed a step ahead of any serious injury during his entire career. An ankle sprain, a broken finger on his non-throwing hand—nothing that kept him out for long.

They saw their counterparts coming at them, and they stopped a few feet from each other. The midfield gathering was starting to look like a convention with the much-larger-than-usual entourage. The array of uniformed officials also included the former player, a league official, a guest coin tosser, and two executives from companies that had paid quite a bit to be there. The latter was Scranton's idea. Each home game representatives from a company that donated money to the Stormcats' charity foundation were allowed on the field for the privilege of watching the toss. Part of the fee went to the team for a scoreboard introduction, which the executives saw as advertising space. Scranton saw it as another way to keep the cash coming in.

The Stormcats won the toss and elected to kick. Gantriel always preferred getting the ball first in the second half.

The players returned to the sidelines.

"The old guy is really alive?" someone asked.

"Barely," replied Canton.

They gathered, and Gantriel let the captains do the motivating.

Balany: "Let's start it off right boys, take it to 'em, right now, everybody feel good? Let's take it to 'em."

Canton was more forceful and succinct with his words. "Sixty minutes! All up for sixty minutes, on three one two three SIXTYMINUTES!"

The Stormcats yelled and whooped and cheered in one bobbing mass of green and white, and the crowd cheered louder as the special teams took the field.

Art Polsky boomed the ball into the end zone, and the teams trotted out to the Explorers' end of the field.

The Stormcats' defense huddled briefly on the sidelines, a jittery group ready for their first hits to get them in the groove of the game. The coaches let them be. From here on they were Canton's team. It wasn't enough for the coaches to draw up plays and assignments; they needed a leader on the field, and Canton was it.

"Our game!" Canton yelled at his corps. "Our game, our season, right now, let's go!"

The linemen and linebackers and the cornerbacks raced onto the field. This was a key year for the Stormcats, but the defense in particular. Gantriel had altered the defensive lineup: In preseason he experimented with setting up two linebackers and using a third rover to play in on run plays or further back on the pass. The team's unit dictated it. Rotinom and Canton were up to the challenge. But there was a dropoff in talent to a third linebacker, coming off an injury. So they went with two, Rotinom and Canton sharing the field.

The Explorers broke their huddle and approached the line of scrimmage. Their quarterback looked warily to his left and right.

"Two! Two-eighteen!" the quarterback barked. "Two! Hut…"

Canton shifted his feet, doing a slow-motion dance. Rotinom didn't move.

"HUT!"

It was as if Rotinom saw himself at a track meet. He sprinted straight into the line of scrimmage before the running back could even make his first move, hitting him square on and driving him down. Loss of one.

The Stormcats all surrounded Rotinom and helped him to his feet, though he didn't need any assistance.

"YEAH!"

"Way to hit big guy!"

"Nice start 99."

Gantriel and Cy Francis just looked at each other. Fans hollered as they settled into their seats.

Canton regrouped them. Field position was everything in football, at any level. Keep an opponent pinned on defense and you are helping your own offense. That's how Canton saw his job.

The Kansas City quarterback called the play, this time a pitchout to the same halfback. His fullback ran ahead of him as a blocker as he took the pitch and tried to skirt wide. This time it was the fullback who was knocked over. He caused Rotinom to stumble some, but the seven-four behemoth still managed to reach out and get a hand on the halfback's jersey, throwing him off balance and slowing him. He looked like a clumsy ballet dancer for just a second. That was enough for three other Stormcats to make the tackle. Gain of two.

Canton pulled his unit together. "They go to the air now, boys, watch pass, pass!"

As expected, the Kansas City quarterback dropped straight back as his receivers ran crossing routes over the middle. He spotted his left flank and fired. But a split-second before he did, Rotinom caught the receiver's path in his peripheral vision, and he sprinted 5 yards to his right.

Just as the quarterback threw, Rotinom leaped. The pass was a perfect shot, and right on target—had Rotinom's outstretched hand not been there. The ball fell, the play ended, and the punting unit quickly took the field.

Gantriel and Francis looked at each other again. Gantriel remained stoic, but Francis couldn't resist a small smile.

The defense huddled around Rotinom as they jogged to the sidelines, exchanging places with the special-teams unit. The Kansas City punter hit a beaut, and after a short runback Cleveland got the ball at their own 35.

Rotinom stopped before the bench and looked to stand, until he saw his teammates sitting, so he joined them. He kept his helmet on and his head down, and he didn't say a word.

Before moving to his squad, Francis sidled up to Gantriel, who eyed Rotinom.

"Guess we know he's the real deal," Francis said.

"We still have a long way to go," Gantriel said, but privately he was relieved.

And in his suite, Brooks Scranton sat and breathed the biggest sigh of relief in the stadium. He swirled his drink, letting the ice rattle just as a way to release some nerves. Inside, he was ecstatic. Things were working. The throng around him of various sponsors and friends of the team clapped and patted him on the back with congratulations.

"Hey, it's only the first series," he said, and they laughed as if it were the funniest joke they had ever heard.

Doc Daugava preferred to watch at home, but he and Scranton agreed it would be best for him to be at the stadium. This way he wouldn't have to make his way downtown to pick up his nephew after the game. Rotinom did not drive and showed no interest in learning. Scranton arranged for

Daugava to watch from his office. Daugava fingered the credential that hung around his neck as he watched the play on the field. Not having grown up around American football, it was a sight. Scranton sensed it.

"You can't quite imagine all this until you actually see it, right?" he said.

"No," Daugava said. "You can't. The..." He searched for the right word. "... pageantry is something else."

"Like soccer growing up for you?" Scranton asked.

"I could not say, Mr. Scranton," Daugava said. "I spent more time with my books than on a playing field."

"That's a good thing," Scranton said.

And in the press box, Catharine flipped a page in her notebook, wrote a capital "R" in the margin, and took notes. Her margin notations led her to find her shorthand notes faster—G for game, I for injury, and now R for Rotinom. She kept a play-by-play on the big man's performance.

R—tkl straight on -1 on 32

R—tkl on 32 pitch left

R—bat pass right

Later, when the game was a jumble of facts and plays and passes and penalties, she could sort out quickly what she needed. If a player was injured, she could easily recall the movement and motion on the field to write about it.

Each quarter a team worker handed out play-by-play sheets, helpful when it came to individual tallies. How many passes were thrown to a certain receiver, how many turnovers were committed, and on and on.

On the field, Balany huddled the team and began to direct the offense. Or rather, Gantriel's offense. The coach and quarterback had an understanding: Gantriel and his offensive coordinator would set the game plan, and Balany would follow it play for play. But Balany was the one with the best view of the opponents' defense, and he was allowed to change as he saw fit. Just not too often.

The Stormcats broke the huddle and marched to the scrimmage line. A fake to Thomas and pitchout to Carver gained 4 yards. Second down saw another fake to Thomas and a short toss to Culpepper, who was open in the flat. The big Georgian trudged for 6 yards and a first down. On the next play, Balany shoved the ball into Thomas' gut, and the fullback charged for 8 yards.

"Figured you were getting tired of the fakes," Balany grinned back in the huddle.

"I was," said the serious Thomas.

"OK boys, let's keep it going," Balany said. "Trips right, 30, go on two—ready? Break!"

The teams lined up, with the Stormcats sending Wisgenti, LeBon and Culpepper all wide to the right side. Balany took the snap and faded three steps, letting the receivers start their routes to draw the defense deep. He waited a second and then, all of a sudden, he turned to his left and tossed a short but sharp pass to Carver, who took it in and turned up field. He ran about 5 yards and juked a defender, cutting inside until two defenders lunged at him, knocking him off balance. Gain of 12.

The Stormcats' alternating offense between runs and short passes had thrown Kansas City off its game, enough to have the ball at the Explorers' 36. Balany sent LeBon and Wisgenti wide again, and went for it all. Carver and Thomas stayed in to help protect the quarterback, and Culpepper drew the defense into the middle. The only person who wasn't decoying anyone was LeBon, who turned his position into a track meet. Balany hit him in stride down the line, and the Stormcats were on the board. To prove he didn't want to fool around, Gantriel signaled to go for a two-point conversion, and Thomas pushed through the middle, giving the Stormcats an 8-0 lead.

LeBon took a hit of oxygen on the sidelines as players congratulated him. Francis rounded up his unit and sent them back out, screaming words of encouragement.

"Plug the holes!" he yelled to Canton. "Stop 'em!" It would be one of his more eloquent comments during the game. Francis was old school, and the emotions of the game always got to him. Sometimes in close games, he would bark out unintelligible commands, once screaming, "Notta Notta Gen Go!" No one knew what he was referring to. A rookie actually had leaned in to ask him what he meant, but Canton pulled him away, saying: "Let him go. He's on a roll. It's his own language."

Stop them they did. On the first play Rotinom and Canton joined in and pounded the Kansas City running back, allowing only a short gain. On second down, Canton heard the audible. It was only the second series of the game for Kansas City, but the Explorer quarterback, already frustrated at his team's inability to move the ball on the ground, would try to pass.

Canton screamed the code for blitz—"Casey! Casey!" But he didn't have to. Rotinom already had crept within a few feet of the line of scrimmage, moving his giant legs gingerly.

"Two! Two!" the Explorer quarterback yelled, one of his receivers moving in motion behind him to the other side of the field. "Two—forty-eight!" HUT!"

He took the snap and started to fade, but it was no use. He couldn't even get out of the pocket, the usually protected area where a quarterback sets to throw. Rotinom hit him first, with Canton joining in for good measure. Both crashed through untouched, and the quarterback crumpled.

Later, when Canton looked back on the season, it would be this play that he would remember as the most important one he and Rotinom would be in on together. He would run the play through his head, remembering pushing down on the ground as he got up. He remembered looking up and seeing Rotinom walk back to the defensive huddle. And he would remember a lot more.

The defense swarmed around the two linebackers. The crowd went crazy. A blitz is always a gamble. If the defenders—usually the linebackers—don't get through, get caught up somehow in the line of scrimmage—receivers can be left with a barren field; no one is there to cover them. But when it works, when the timing is just right, it's a play that leaves the quarterback in a crushed heap for a loss of yards.

And that's how play continued. The only time the Explorers could move the ball was when they faked a handoff to a running back and threw. The better the fake, the more Rotinom was fooled. But it didn't matter. Carver scored late in the first half, and Galveston Gruene ran back an interception in the second half, adding to Kansas City's unfolding nightmare. With one of two conversions made—Gantriel rarely went for extra-point kicks—the Stormcats had a 22-0 lead and never looked back.

With a minute to play, Andrews and Trent joined the cattle line to head to the lockers. And true to his word, Scranton let the team celebrate, not showing up after the game. Daugava had watched the game silently, sipping tea while Scranton's suite filled with gregarious friends.

"So, he played well?" Daugava asked Scranton. "I am

sorry, I am still understanding football, the…" the doctor searched for the correct word. "…nuances of the game."

The owner smiled. "He played very well. Extremely well. The media will want to talk to him now—can he handle that?"

"To a degree," Daugava said. "He is, as you know, a shy boy."

Scranton nodded. "I'll see you are in the parking lot to take him away as soon as possible."

In the lockers, chaos reigned but only briefly. Trent made his way to Kansas City's locker room to hear the coach's postgame comments as players showered, while Andrews listened to Gantriel in the outer area for the media.

"…Kansas City was difficult to prepare for. They can come at you in so many ways. I thought we stuck to our game plan, though, and I was pleased with our defense being able to react as well as they did." Gantriel finished his overall and always brief comments with a slight grimace, as if he were a sick child whose time had come to take his medicine.

Reporter: "Coach, 99—Rotinom—he was in on many stops, run and pass. Where did he come from?"

"Riga Rotinom came to us as a free agent late in training camp. One of our scouts, I believe, saw him first. I thought he had a remarkable first game."

Reporter: "He crept up the depth chart pretty fast. Is his ability the reason you changed the defense from a four-three to a five-two?"

"Partly. We just feel he and Canton can cover a lot of ground, and it frees us up to add a body, either on the line or as a defensive back. I thought the defense as a whole did a decent job of reacting to the ball, picking up the run or the pass. The coaches worked hard preparing them this week...."

Andrews jumped in as soon as he took a breath. She always knew when Gantriel was done answering a question and resorted to rambling. "Coach, back to Rotinom for a sec. When he showed up in camp, and he hadn't played before, what was the first thing that went though your mind?"

Andrews couldn't place it, but something in Gantriel's face changed. She had struck a chord of some sort. But just as fast as she saw it, it was gone.

"His size and preparation, paired with his speed and agility, made us want to take a look at him. His practices were productive. He responded well..."

Gantriel quickly turned back into coachspeak; he spoke it fluently.

A television reporter chimed in: "Seventeen tackles, coach, seventeen. Pretty good game."

Andrews rolled her eyes and sighed to herself. Sometimes TV folks often didn't exactly state a question, they just said something from the game, and the coach would ramble on a bit. If a coach were in a bad mood, though, you had better make sure you asked an actual question. Andrews took down what he said, listened to the follow-ups, then the press conference broke up and the reporters made their way into the lockers.

After a win, the mood of a locker room was light. Players would talk a bit freer, laugh and smile more. And when the win was a solid win, a shutout—meaning both offense and defense did their jobs—well, it could be downright giddy. When the doors opened for the reporters, most players were dressed, some wore towels. A few stragglers were heading to the showers. The carpet was littered with jerseys, jock straps and socks. The clubhouse guys would have their hands full picking up the assorted strewn attire for laundry.

"Baby you see that pick?" Gruene was saying to any teammates who walked by. "Right there. I couldn't have ordered it any better!"

The five-foot-ten defensive back relished the moment and was hamming it up. His teammates didn't mind. Someone tossed a towel to him, which hit him in the shoulder and fell to the floor.

"Hey, you get that pigskin OK but can't nab a towel?" someone said, players laughing.

Reporters often make a beeline for the star of the game. No way could a station not get a soundbite from the guy who scored the winning touchdown, or recovered a key fumble, or who set a record. Today was no different, except for the fact reporters have a general idea where the guy's locker is. Today they didn't. They all scanned the numbers above the lockers for "99."

They found it, in the back, near other rookies. It was barren and clean, except for a gym bag inside with a pair of cleats on the ground. And Rotinom was gone.

CHAPTER 13

The tiny green icon for "phone" buzzed and blinked on virtually every cell phone in the Stormcats' offices Monday morning. Sails had the most messages, but Scranton wasn't far behind. Andrews called each once, then drove out to Daugava's again.

She and Trent didn't need an editor to tell them what had to be done before the next game. Someone had to talk to Rotinom—now. So she drove through the tree-lined streets of the old neighborhood once more and pulled up near Daugava's home. She rang the buzzer, got no answer, and went back to her car. Stakeout time.

"It's a nice day, Doc, you gotta get out sometime," she said to herself as she tapped her steering wheel. She waited, alternating her time by researching the injuries that had occurred in Sunday games and glancing at Daugava's door. There was no side gate; if there were a back door she couldn't see it. It was just a matter of waiting.

The players had most of Monday off. It was a day to heal from Sunday's collisions. In the afternoon, they would have a film session breaking down the game, then many of the guys would get together to watch the night game. It was one of the only times players could watch professional football in the regular season. Gantriel would run through every play of the entire game on film—actually video but for old time's sake it was still called film—then they were free to go while the coaches would start analyzing next week's opponent. Then everyone would come back Tuesday refreshed. Hopefully.

Andrews' editor, Todd Kelly, was in a foul mood Monday morning when he reviewed coverage of the game with no quotes from the game's star. He knew no one else got to Rotinom, but it didn't lessen his mood. In fact, one of the calls to the Stormcats offices that morning was from him— not for interview requests but a reminder on league policy about making players available after games. Scranton would have to talk to Daugava about that.

Andrews was done looking up the latest injury reports, which were filed daily by the league, and she propped her notebook on the steering wheel of her hybrid car. She hated stakeouts but knew when she was on one it was for a key interview. She watched cars go by and saw a rare, darkened puff from an exhaust pipe. Auto-emission laws had gotten tighter over the years, and car companies had invented better exhaust filters. So it wasn't often you saw fumes belching from cars. She got out to stretch and saw a woman coming out of the apartment building.

"Excuse me, ma'am, I'm looking for Dr. Daugava. Do you know him? I think he's your neighbor."

"Doctor, huh? He do something bad to you?"

"Uh, no, not exactly," Andrews said. "He's just a tough guy to locate."

"Probably overbilled you. I can't stand dealing with them pompous asses."

Andrews nodded out of politeness and let her continue.

"It's probably that little guy who's always with the big guy.

I mean HUGE. That guy must be eight feet tall."

"Yes," Andrews said. "That's the guy. I heard he has a nephew living with him."

"Only seen 'em a couple of times," she said. "He's real quiet."

"The doctor?" Andrews said.

"Yeah, but the big guy—who'd you say he was, his nephew? Yeah, he's quiet too."

It wasn't much, but at least Andrews now had figured that Rotinom probably lived with his uncle. How long would that last after he got a fat contract?

After that, Andrews walked to a diner she had driven past. Maybe someone there knew the doctor, she thought, knowing she was reaching at straws.

Inside the apartment, Daugava had gotten off the phone with Scranton, who apologized for not telling Doc about the league rules on talking to players. Daugava said he understood and would take care of it. When he hung up, he looked at the business card on his table, from the young reporter who had stopped him in the parking lot.

"Well," he said to no one, "maybe it is time Miss Andrews and I talk a little."

Andrews had settled in to a worn vinyl seat and ordered coffee when her phone rang. She couldn't believe it. It was Daugava, apologizing for not having time to talk earlier but willing to meet with her. Flustered, she told him she happened to be at the nearby diner, leaving out the part she had sat outside his apartment waiting for him. He said he would be down in a few minutes.

When the diminutive man walked in he was, as usual, dressed in a white shirt and thin black tie, black pants and shoes. He took off his hat as he approached.

"Miss Andrews, how are you?" he asked.

"Fine, Doctor, fine. Thanks for coming. I, uh, rang your door earlier."

"How fortuitous," Daugava said. "The buzzer, though, it doesn't work."

"Ah," said Andrews, now realizing why Daugava was home all this time.

A waitress came over and put a cup of tea in front of Daugava.

"Here you are, Doc," she said, smiling. "Usually don't see you in here so early."

"Yes, yes, a bit early today," he said.

Doc ordered a Reuben and Andrews chose a club sandwich. The waitress laid down small napkins but no utensils; restaurants had gotten smart about conserving water and washing only what was needed. Gone were the days of a spoon, fork and knife wrapped in a paper napkin and tied by a paper holder.

"First names with waitresses, Doc—come here often?"

"Yes, a nice place, and I am not much of a cook."

"Doctor," Andrews said, "after a game, players usually stick around to —"

"Yes, yes, I know," he said, cutting her off. "Riga, my nephew, should have stayed to answer questions. It is required. I am sorry. He is shy, despite his size."

"Actually," she said, "I was going to say, after a game, a good game—a great game by a particular player, they want to stay. They get a little limelight, it airs on all the stations, it's everywhere online, their name is published—and not next to a crime report. It's all good news—do you understand Doc?"

"I do. Riga is not like that. He just enjoys playing football, but he spends a lot of time alone. He doesn't have much of an ego."

"What does he do? Let me guess—video games."

Daugava smiled. "No, no games. He reads."

"Well, Doc, he reads, and I write. Sounds like a good mix. Speaking of writing, I am working on a story…" Andrews segued into the disclaimer she had to get across early and clearly in every sitdown, that she was a reporter working on a story. "What does he like to read?"

"History, mostly, current events, American civics—he is still learning about this country, you know."

"Tell me about that—how long have you two been here?" Andrews was trying to contain herself and keep the questions coming one at a time.

"I have been here for many years, but Riga is new here, barely a year."

"Do you work around here?" Andrews asked.

"No," he replied. "I am an engineer—well, retired. I took a buyout several years ago."

"I had an uncle who was an engineer," she said. "Electrical, I think."

"Yes, that is what I am," Daugava replied.

"Don't know anything about it; the 'words' part of my brain works better than the 'numbers' side."

He smiled, and she continued. "Why did he come to this country now?"

"Because the only football in Riga is one you kick," he said.

Now Andrews smiled. She was entitled to a dumb question now and then.

"So Riga—how did he come to be named after the city?"

"My sister and brother-in-law were proud of their home

city, so they named him after it," Daugava said.

"Where are they now?"

"They were killed in a car accident when Riga was a baby. Riga did not know them."

Andrews looked up. Her mother had died young but she had a father who was around for her, and who she was close to.

"That must have been difficult—in an orphanage?"

Daugava nodded. "It was well run, a good school. Riga enjoyed—enjoys—learning."

"But no parents," Andrews said.

"No, sadly," Daugava said.

"Why didn't you take him sooner? Not that you had to, I just mean—"

"It is all right," he said. "I could not, with my personal situation, care better than the orphanage people. Riga was going to go to university, but the orphanage burned, and he had no place to live. So I went and got him."

Andrews let it go. She didn't want to scare him off.

"So, Riga gets involved in football in Latvia. How does that happen?"

"I asked Riga that when I visited a couple of years ago. Apparently there was one football in an athletic closet, a donation with assorted equipment. Riga was the only one who picked it up. Everyone else went for the other 'footballs,' " Daugava said, smiling.

"But how did he learn the sport? You can't just take a football from a broom closet and the next day dominate on a professional field," she said.

"Well, he read, he saw video, and he was able to get a few of the boys to indulge his sport. Riga would direct the other kids a bit. The whole time Riga was working out, staying in shape. He wrote me about this, but I had no idea how good of shape he was in, or how big he had grown."

"Were his parents, well, large, like him?" Andrews said.

"Yes, my brother-in-law was much taller than me, and his wife, my sister, was almost taller. She played volleyball—not for the Olympics or anything like that, but she coached children."

Andrews jumped through her many questions, now realizing Doc must have been the one to make the introductions to the Stormcats. "So let me understand something—the Stormcats, they took a flier on your nephew?"

"A flier?" Daugava asked, taking a bite of Reuben, thousand-island dressing dribbling off the Rye toast.

"A chance—a wild chance based on a guess rather than facts."

"Ah, yes. I had some video of Riga working out, I showed it to Mr. Scranton."

"Do—do you still have that video?" Andrews asked. "I would love to see that, be able to share that with readers."

Daugava thought for a moment. "Yes, I can send it to you. But it is Riga working out alone. Nothing exciting."

Andrews thought carefully about her next question as she finished her club sandwich. "I would like a one-on-one interview with Riga. He is an interesting guy."

"Miss Andrews, I tell you, he is shy, very shy. You see this aggressive person on the football field. He is quiet alone, reading. But I promise this: In the locker room, he will stay after games to answer questions."

Andrews held back her disappointment. There was a huge difference in grabbing a player at his locker after a game for an interview and getting a sitdown with him. In the first scenario, it was a quick, communal-type experience. Everyone was hearing—and using—the same quotes, and the questions usually were almost always on the game itself. But with a sitdown, the pace was more leisurely, and the reporter and player had a chance to discuss in depth other issues. That, unfortunately, didn't seem likely. But Andrews wouldn't quit.

"Doc, is there anything else you can tell me about Riga? Anything I haven't asked?"

"No, like I said, he is very private."

"Doc, I appreciate your time, and I would like to talk to you again some time."

Daugava thought for a moment. The questions hadn't been as difficult to field as he thought. He didn't want to continue them, but if they kept Andrews from Rotinom, it might be worth it.

"Oh, and I would appreciate seeing that video. Readers would love to see a younger Rotinom working out." And so would my editor, she thought.

"I will do that, Miss Andrews."

"Thanks, Doc—much appreciated." She waved a credit card near an old scanner, grabbed her notes, and they headed to the door.

"I am going to go this way," Daugava said. "I have a stop to make."

Andrews nodded and shook his hand. "Thanks again, Doc," and turned in the opposite direction toward her car. She stayed calm and professional on the outside, but inside she was jumping. The first bit of real news on this guy, and she had it. No one else.

CHAPTER 14

The players watched the stop-and-start of the film on Kansas City until their eyes blinked and butts hurt from the hard chairs in the theater. It was a good session, but in an odd way Gantriel didn't like it. When there were problems, there was something concrete to point out. This was a lopsided game, and he wanted to focus on the negatives to fix things. With lowly Nashville coming up Sunday, he didn't want a team that was too cocky and would let its guard down.

After film several of the players changed and broke for ajo, hopping on Mondays because of giant screens that resembled ones from old movie theaters but with high resolution. The comfortable setting was drawing more and more people, football fans and non-fans alike. As the players walked, guitar chords from a jukebox cut through the restaurant and bar as TV screens showed repeated talking heads in pregame mode without sound. When it got closer to game time the TV volume would turn up, the juke would be turned off, and the players would be settled into their private booth with a screen nearby. Though new, ajo already was drawing quite a crowd—from sports fans to business people to out-of-town guests. Business was great.

In a doorway to the back, Adam stood, nodding. Olivia crossed her arms, looking over the crowd with stern approval. Julia smiled.

Half the Stormcat group headed for the video-racing game while the other half headed for the booth, fielding an autograph seeker or two along the way. Olivia almost stepped in to make sure the fans didn't get too annoying, but Balany's slight nod in her direction said it was OK.

"Hey," Wisgenti said to McAdams as they took their seats, "did you hear about the bank teller who got locked in the bank safe?"

McAdams shook his head no.

"Yeah, he apologized to the bank president because he said it was really his vault."

LeBon groaned. McAdams stared.

"What?" McAdams said.

"Tell you later," LeBon said.

Balany turned the subject to football, as he always did at one point or another on their nights out.

"Everyone ready for Nashville? Carver, you got your legs yet buddy? Feel like running?"

"Born ready, sir, ready to go," the running back said.

Canton joined his teammates, the lone defensive representative among the offensive group.

"What's up with your d-side teammates?" Balany asked.

"Slumming?" LeBon chipped in.

"Thought I'd raise the IQ level a few points," Canton said.

"Well tell us a joke," McAdams said. " 'cause Wisgenti's are bad."

"Look," said Wisgenti, "just remember what Shakespeare said about football. He thought it was easy. His exact words were 'It's not bard.' "

Eyes turned toward him. McAdams was the first to speak up.

"Wait a minute, they didn't have football when Shakespeare was around.... Did they?"

"So," Balany said, turning to Canton and ignoring McAdams' inability to get Wisgenti's jokes. "We gonna see another two-man show Sunday?"

"What do you mean?" Canton asked.

"Well," the quarterback said, "you finished with what—seven tackles? Who would have guessed you wouldn't have led the game with seven? The big guy's a machine out there. I guess I didn't even realize it until I saw the film today."

Canton took a sip of beer. "He's amazing. He makes the rest of us look like we're running in place."

"Fine by me," Balany said. "You guys pinned them so many times I was ready to change my address to the red zone."

Culpepper crashed into his seat, Thomas sitting next to him.

"How'd you do?" McAdams asked.

"Lost it before I got to the mountain stage," he said.

McAdams smiled. He had gone further in the racing game. "Never bring a boy to do a man's job."

"Carver," Balany piped up, "what's the word of the day?"

"The word of the day, gents, is 'ersatz,' " said Carver, the lover of language.

"Er-what?" asked McAdams.

"Ersatz," repeated Carver.

"Fake," Thomas said.

Carver nodded to his backfield mate. "Yeah, a substitute, inferior. Bad imitation."

"What is that, French?" asked Balany.

"Yeah, is it, Frenchy?" McAdams repeated, turning to LeBon.

"Don't know, and I'm not French," the receiver said.

"German," said Carver.

"I'm not German, either," LeBon said.

Just then Balany's phone chirped two short bursts, followed by two more. It was a notify that something had moved online about the Stormcats. He had programmed it to alert him with any breaking news, knowing that while players often found out from the team first about various happenings, every now and then a reporter would come up with something before the front office could get word to them.

Catharine Andrews' dispatch popped up on Balany's phone via The American's online notification:

Catharine Payton Andrews / The American / Cleveland:

At seven feet, four inches, Riga Rotinom could not be missed by anyone in Emerald Lake Stadium last Sunday. Especially not by the Kansas City running backs and receivers, who were smashed with an incessant pounding all day from the rookie and veteran Tiger Canton. Rotinom's 17 tackles, which broke a team record, helped the Stormcat offense gain field position all afternoon. But Rotinom's on-field aggression belies his off-field nature, according to the man who knows him best. Dr. Janis Daugava, the big man's uncle, says Rotinom—named after the city in Latvia where he was born—enjoys spending time alone, reading history…

Balany finished the story while the players chatted.

"Guys," he said. "Check this out."

Balany clicked on the video link, and a grainy video appeared, showing Rotinom working out—alone, but pushing a sled farther than any of the players had seen, running agility drills quicker than anyone, and racing wind sprints faster than someone his size should be able to move.

"Would have surprised me before I saw him on the field," Canton said. "The guy can bring it."

"I'll say," Carver said, remembering the time he was dinged during practice.

The game of the week popped on, and the analysts on television suddenly had voices.

"Hey, what is his deal, Canton? He was gone after the game."

"Don't know," Canton said. "Guy isn't exactly cold, but he's quiet, man, says two words at most."

"OK by me, if he keeps hitting the way he's hitting," Balany said. "Man's just doing his job. But you figure he might want to take in a little break every now and then, join us once in a blue moon."

"Wonder what he's doing now," someone said.

"You heard the story," Canton said. "Reading. And I believe it, cause I know he's read the playbook. When he left the other day he was reading it as he walked out the door. Guy lives it. Coaches must love him."

"Where's Latvia?" someone said.

"In the Baltics," Thomas replied.

"That helps," Culpepper said.

Thomas sighed. "It's between Estonia and Lithuania."

Balany searched on his phone and quickly found basic information on the country. "Says here it's about the size of West Virginia," he said. "Capital, Riga."

"He's about as big as West Virginia," Culpepper said.

The game kicked off, and they turned their attention to the screen above them, getting lost as they watched their brethren.

Meanwhile, in the modest apartment on the East Side of town, Daugava worked at his table, engineering books open, notes scattered. Various diagrams he had sketched showed parallel lines winding their way into what looked like a jumbled knot. He held a pair of tweezers in one hand and a pair of wires, red and black, in the other. He was, at heart, a scientist, and always would be, and tinkering kept him at ease. And in a bedroom, with no television and little furniture, Rotinom sat still, the darkness surrounding him.

CHAPTER 15

Sunday morning arrived with a slightly cool breeze; summer finally was giving way to fall. Leaves hadn't turned, but the warm temperatures were dropping as players arrived for taping sessions and any medical attention they needed. The Nashville team, which had flown in the night before—all teams flew the day before games, per league rules—was doing the same in their locker room. Nashville had won only four games last year, and had started the season with a loss. They needed to get on track.

But the Stormcats had two things going for them—their health and, after last week's trouncing of Kansas City, confidence. They knew they could get it done.

When Balany was on, he was unstoppable. And on this Sunday afternoon, he was on. He directed the offense with precision, alternating runs and passes. Wisgenti and LeBon ran crisp routes and pulled in three touchdowns between them. Carver broke 100 yards again, capped by a magnificent 60-yard run on third down from his own 40. He took the handoff and ran three steps, then dug in his right foot and changed direction to the left, put on the gas and was off. Once he beat the offensive line, only a defensive back got near him but it was no use. He stiff-armed him and raced into the end zone. On the sideline, Nashville's coaches were livid over their blown coverage, with at least two hats and a tablet slammed into the ground.

On defense, it was the Rotinom-Canton show again.

Canton plugged up holes and was in on conceivably every play he could contribute. Rotinom's speed on defense and strength simply overpowered anyone near him. Nashville's only hope was trying to decoy the defense by showing a run play, then throwing long. They got a touchdown and a field goal out of plays like this, which worried Gantriel. It was a small chink in the armor. If a lowly team like Nashville could get six on them with a simple fake and deep pass, what would a better team do? Still, though, the Stormcats plugged the run well. Rotinom batted four passes and was in on fifteen stops. The Nashville running back, fresh and cocky at kickoff, looked wobbly and shaken by the end of the game. On one play Rotinom changed direction as fast as the Nashville back did, and he stopped him in his tracks by planting him in the grass in his own backfield. The crowd loved it.

Gantriel took him out with the score 27-10 late in the fourth, finding some playing time for a linebacker further down on the depth chart. Unfortunately, after Rotinom, the understudy looked like he was moving in slow-motion.

And in his suite, Scranton was breathing easier on each play, never tiring of the occasional "Where did you find this guy?" queries. He'd laugh it off, finding a different answer every time—"The Latvia Developmental League, ha"—then left to chat with Doc.

The player, doctor and owner agreed to Rotinom's contract, which recognized Daugava as legal guardian. His salary went directly to the doctor, who stashed some of it in a Cleveland bank, but the majority went to an overseas account.

"Doc," Scranton said, "I have to admit, I simply don't like to take chances on unproven talent. I didn't stop worrying until he made his first tackle in the first game. Now, seeing him repeat that performance here…" He let his voice trail.

"He is a very good player, then, he knows the playbook?" Daugava said.

Scranton looked at him. "It's more than a playbook, Doc. These guys give their heart out there. You can know the playbook, but you have to have the size and the stamina and the speed and the smarts. What we look for when we evaluate players is as many of those attributes as possible. Few ever have it all."

"But Riga does, yes?" the doctor said.

Scranton sipped his drink. "Yes, he does. I don't know how you did it or understand it. But he's—do you realize in two games he has made 32 tackles?"

Daugava stared. "Very good, I take it?"

Scranton smiled. "Doc, many players go through an entire season without that many."

Daugava sat back and also relaxed. He, like Scranton, had been nervous at the beginning, but that anxiety had faded.

Scranton called in an assistant. "Renee, would you accompany Dr. Daugava to the postgame room. He is going to watch interviews and go into the locker room."

"Of course, Mr. Scranton."

A woman with a tight ponytail and the Stormcats' logo on a golf shirt appeared in the doorway. The man who had spent the afternoon watching Rotinom from afar now would watch him react to the media up close.

CHAPTER 16

By the time Renee and Daugava wound their way through the labyrinth of elevators and long corridors to the postgame room, Gantriel already was in full coachspeak. "...We let our guard down on occasion and we'll have to work on that. Nashville is a better team than people say. My hat's off to them. I'm just glad we came out healthy, not too battered and bruised..."

Daugava listened intently, then let Renee guide him to a far corner, where he could watch reporters ask specific questions about the game. Has Carver's knee completely healed, in light of his performance? Did he envision having a line-backer with more than 30 tackles after the second game of the season? How much of his game plan is Balany sticking to, how much is he changing during the game? And so on.

Renee led him into the lockers and pointed out a quick tour: The coaches' offices, training rooms, hallway that led to the weight room. Daugava was amazed at the spaciousness of the lockers. When he was a boy his father played soccer in Latvia. He took Janis into a locker room after a game to meet some of the players. Janis remembered a damp, wooden room—a warped, pine bench; a hard, cold concrete floor; and the constant drip of leaky faucets. This was nothing like that. Players had large, individual open closets with recliners, and a varnished bench that ran along the lockers. He saw more headphones and game-console units than clothes hanging in the closets. Along one wall were large mesh bins with jerseys and underwear in them, draped over them, and on the floor around them. Renee told the doctor about how the locker-room staff would have to stay hours after each game and practice to wash everything.

"It takes a lot of people to keep things moving here," she said.

"Yes, I believe it does," he said, surveying the room, still gripping his briefcase as his eyes moved along the numbers and names atop the lockers. She positioned him close, but not too close, to Rotinom, whose eye caught him briefly. Daugava nodded slightly and smiled. Then the doors rushed open and Rotinom sat by his locker, a crush of lights and poles and lenses and people coming directly at him. He was already dressed and sitting at the bench in front of his locker as the media swarmed. Despite Rotinom's size, Daugava could barely see him.

The questions fired immediately, in a rush like a wave hitting a beach. Andrews squirmed her way to the front, a TV cameraman's microphone pole clipping her knee as she inched forward.

"Riga, what about the game? Thirty-two tackles in two games? Did you expect the NPL to be like this? Where did you play football before? Riga, your thoughts right now…

The questions kept coming, and Riga blinked at the lights. He answered in his deliberate and careful and boring way, until almost all of the reporters had gone. TV barely had any soundbites from him worth using. Riga Rotinom, it seemed, might be a monster on the field, but off of it he was not flashy at all.

The reporters went off for Balany and Carver and Canton and the receivers, and Rotinom—with the same emotion he had shown when answering questions—picked up his bag and made his way to the door. Daugava thanked Renee, put on his cap and started to follow. Just then Andrews ran up to the big linebacker, who was almost at the door.

"Riga, I'm Catharine Andrews of The American. Do you miss Latvia?"

The words tumbled out quickly. She wanted his attention and she had it, finally.

Rotinom turned and thought for a moment, staring at her from several feet away. In her first face-to-face, she expected him to be intimidating, but he wasn't, despite his size.

"Latvia is my home. But I like it here."

"I spoke to your uncle. He said you learned the game on your own, trained on your own. Did you have any help?"

Again Riga stared at her for a second, then answered: "No help. I read. Books, training on my own."

Andrews moved closer and continued: "Riga, what book are you reading now?"

Rotinom didn't answer. Andrews felt a gentle hand on her elbow. "Miss Andrews, good to see you again,"

Daugava said.

"Doc, I was just—"

"Yes, yes, Riga was asked many questions today—he answered them, yes?"

"Yes, he did Doc. Thanks—what are you doing here?"

"I came to pick up Riga," he said, then, looking around as if he were about to tell a secret, "I believe my nephew is the only player on the team who doesn't have driver's license."

Andrews laughed. "I'm sure you're right, Doc."

Daugava smiled and doffed his cap. "Have a good day, Miss Andrews, and by the way, I enjoyed your story the other day."

"Thanks Doc, she said, whirling back to the crush of players finishing showers and getting dressed.

With that the dapper little man was off, headed to the same door in the back of the locker room where Rotinom had gone through. It took Andrews about a minute to realize the linebacker had stealthed off and never answered her last question.

Later, on the elevator, the quips started immediately. An old columnist said to anyone who would listen, "We waited for THAT?"

"If you had trouble keeping up with him, my notes are pretty good."

"Wonder if he's going to be this boring all the time or just on game days?"

"Can't wait to see him after a loss."

The Cleveland fans would come to love Rotinom's play on the field. The media would too, but pulling more than three-word answers was going to be a chore all season.

CHAPTER 17

The hype started soon, days before the team was to travel to San Jose for its first road game. The "99" jerseys came out, with Sails pushing the marketing division and the legal guys to get the licensing done faster than a two-minute drill. The official ones said "ROTINOM" across the back. The unofficial ones showed "MONSTER" or "BEAST" over the numbers. They all sold. Sails' idea to give a portion of the proceeds to a charity didn't hurt, either. The Stormcats became one of the few teams in the NPL with a defensive player's jersey outselling all of the team's other jerseys, including those from offensive stars like Balany and Carver and the receivers. But it didn't stop there. Coffee mugs came out. Kids' Halloween costumes, women's night shirts and ball caps with the Stormcat logo next to a small "99" all followed.

And the radio talk shows lit up.

"Rotinom, this guy, I don't know where he came from, but he's the answer. He's the guy who's gonna get it done. They should hire two bodyguards to protect him at all times 'cause he is the single reason why this team is winning…."

Andrews snickered. She admired fans' passions to follow a team the way Cleveland fans did, but she also thought they were way too fickle. They jumped on the bandwagon when a player was doing well, praising him with scores of phone calls. One bad game, though, and he was toast, the adulation tossed off the bandwagon and left in a heap without a care.

Fans also had taken to Rotinom financially, through the PLX. The rookie's value was rising dramatically with every tackle, it seemed, as more and more fans wanted to "own" a piece of him.

Andrews flew to San Jose, whose enclosed, climate-controlled stadium was only two years old. The Bays were coming off their first win to even their record at 1-1, and they would be tested against a proven Stormcat team. Cleveland, meanwhile, had its first game on the road, always a challenge.

The game trudged on, neither team gaining an advantage, trading punts. It was a struggle in the trenches, each line becoming grass-stained and blood-stained and bruised in the first half.

But on the Stormcats' first possession of the second quarter, Thomas gained 8 yards because McAdams had leveled his man, and a pass to Carver in the flat threw off the Bays' defense. First down, looking for more. Balany faked a handoff to Carver and threw a perfect spiral to LeBon, who had cut across the middle of the field behind the linebackers. The key to such a pass was its timing, but also the throw itself. If the ball were thrown so the receiver had to leap and miss it, there's a chance the ball could be deflected, and defensive backs would swarm like fish to a bread crumb tossed their way. The pass had to be numbers high or lower, had to be timed to hit the receiver. For his part, the receiver had to have no fear of being slammed while he was looking for the ball.

Balany to LeBon worked. It gained 22 yards, deflated the crowd, and pushed the Stormcats onto the cusp of the red zone, that magical area inside the opponents' 20-yard line. From there Gantriel played it safe, with a run up the middle by Thomas, who churned his way for 8 yards, then Carver juked for four. First and 10 as the Stormcat bench shouted encouragement, willing Balany and the offense to get the ball into the end zone.

"Make a goal baby! Let's go!"

"Get six now, push it in!"

Balany handed off to Thomas, with Carver decoying to his left, and Thomas pushed it in, standing up. Cleveland had struck first. Gantriel stayed true to his game plan and had them go for two, with Culpepper catching a pass in the corner to make it 8-0.

The Bays got it back on the kickoff return.

A speedy rookie tore off for the sidelines and, with good blocks, raced downfield, virtually untouched. Gantriel was stoic on the sidelines, but anyone who saw the menacing albeit quick glance at his special-teams coach knew exactly how irritated he was.

The Bays settled for an extra point, and the teams went to halftime, 8-7.

In the locker room Gantriel was livid about the special teams allowing the touchdown, but he always allowed his players rest time before making any points. He pushed them to catch their blocks, to work harder.

"Our pursuit is for shit!" Gantriel shouted, ignoring the nearby whiteboard. "Make the hits on the runback!"

Then he and his assistants retired again to the visiting coaches' offices for any adjustments that had to be made before the coaches talked to each of their units and checked with the doctor on any injuries.

Rotinom was playing his usual stellar game. His speed made it appear as if he were blitzing on almost every run play.

When the Stormcat defensive line flushed the Bays' quarterback off to the side, Rotinom was right there, leaping to block down a pass. His teammates would tease him in the locker room about having "club hands" since he batted passes regularly but never recorded an interception.

Neither team was advancing the ball much. The Cleveland defense kept San Jose out of field-goal range; that's all it would take for the Bays to gain the lead. Then, late in the game, something happened that would elevate Rotinom even more in the eyes of the fans, his teammates and the coaches.

The Bays slowly put together a drive, moving the ball with fakes and a couple of passes. Rotinom was in on nearly every running play it seemed, but the fakes still threw him off. The Bays came out of the two-minute warning rested, and on third down the San Jose quarterback faked to his fullback and pitched to his running back who ran as far and as fast as he could, knowing three of his teammates were trying to delay Rotinom. He juked a defensive back coming at him, cut and got a first down in Stormcat territory after a 21-yard run. The next two plays were incomplete passes.

On third down, the fullback took the ball and plowed through the line, but he was hit by Canton and fumbled as he was going down. Out of the corner of his eye, the fullback saw the large "99" coming at him from his right, and a teammate—a wide receiver—ran close to him on his left. As the fullback fell near his own sideline, and with the officials' view blocked, he quickly batted the ball to his teammate, who picked it up on the bounce and ran 40-plus yards into the end zone. The crowd went wild; it was the first lead any team had gained on Cleveland all year.

Rotinom trudged back to the huddle since the Bays were going to go for two. Canton looked up at his teammate, who was staring at the field where the play happened.

"Big man, line up, let's go—hey, what is it?"

"Invalid."

"What?" Canton said.

"The play is invalid because of the fumble-advance rule," Rotinom said.

Canton glanced at the Bays, who were moving at a slightly faster speed to get set up for the two-point conversion. If they got the next play called before the Stormcats could issue a challenge, the play would stand. That was the rule. But so far, the only person who questioned the play was Rotinom. It appeared that none of the referees had seen anything wrong.

"What do you mean!" Canton shouted.

Rotinom repeated: "Invalid play."

The Bays were frantically lining up, the quarterback yelling at his receivers to get into position.

"WHAT DO YOU MEAN!?" Canton screamed again.

"If an offensive player loses possession on fourth down, only the fumbling player may recover and or advance the football. A two-minute warning negates the possession requirement. If any player fumbles after a two-minute warning, only the player losing possession may retrieve and or advance the ball. If another offensive player regains the ball, then the ball is spotted at that place," Rotinom said.

Canton stared at him, almost speechless.

"What—did you see—never mind," Canton said as he turned to the Cleveland sideline, waving his arms above his head. When he caught the attention of Coach Francis, Canton grabbed his right wrist with his left hand—the Stormcats' signal to throw the challenge flag.

"Challenge, challenge, challenge!" the captain screamed.

The Bays were almost in position. Francis turned to Gantriel to let him know, but Gantriel had seen Canton's signal. The coach put his hand on the belt clip that held the red flag coaches threw to indicate they wanted the officials to review a play. Gantriel didn't see anything that would merit the challenge, but he reacted quickly, tearing the flag from its clip and throwing it on the field in one motion. The players' on the sidelines did their part, screaming in a choppy unison: "CHALLENGE! CHALLENGE!"

The nearest referee turned and saw it, just as the Bays quarterback was getting set under center to go for the two-point conversion. The referee whistled and waved his arms as the quarterback snapped the ball.

The quarterback angrily shook off his chin strap as he walked to the sidelines to wait for the ruling with his coach. Canton already was on his way to the sidelines to explain to Gantriel and Francis why he had called for the challenge.

"He advanced a fumble," said Canton as he reached the coaches.

"Didn't see it," Gantriel said.

"Neither did I," said Francis.

"And neither did I," Canton agreed. "But Rotinom did. He recited the rule to me chapter and verse, he saw it."

Gantriel looked behind Canton. Rotinom was the lone Stormcat on the field; the rest of the defense was near the sidelines getting water.

"Rotinom!" Gantriel shouted.

The big man lumbered over.

"What did you see on the play?" Gantriel asked.

"On a play from scrimmage, if an offensive player fumbles anywhere on the field —"

"I know the rule," Gantriel cut him off sternly. "What did you see."

Rotinom thought for a second, then said, "Fullback fumbled before he was down, then knocked ball to teammate with less than two minutes to go in the half," Rotinom said.

Francis looks at Gantriel. "I didn't see the advance. I thought it squirted out and 89 was there."

Gantriel then turned to Canton, who shrugged. "I was holding 32 up; I never saw the ball pop out."

The referees then left the small on-field room that served as their review station. The walls were Plexiglas but bannered with logos of sponsors, including a tire company urging fans to "Make the right choice." A referee huddled under a camera as he looked at the angles of the replay. He conferred with his fellow officials briefly, then trotted to midfield, turning on his microphone.

"Upon further review, the offensive player fumbled the ball before he was down, but directed it to a teammate," he said, making a batting motion with his hand. "The ball…"

Even before the ref had finished the ruling the Bays coach was shouting into his microphone and his quarterback was running back on the field. They obviously had planned two contingencies: One play would be called should the play stand, another if it were overruled. The crowd booed. Overturning the play was disastrous for the Bays; it meant not only that they didn't take the lead, but were not within field-goal range. They had no choice but to go for it on fourth down.

Canton called a quick defensive huddle. He had done the math; the Bays needed more than 10 yards to be in field-goal range. They had to pass.

"We got a gift," he said as he surveyed mostly tired faces. "Let's use it."

He widened the distance between himself and Rotinom.

The quarterback made no attempt to cover the fact he was going to throw. He barked his signals from several feet behind center, in shotgun formation. He stood alone, no running backs around.

"Ready—eighty-four—eighty-four hut hut HUT!"

He took the snap and immediately started looking downfield. It was all a guessing game. Canton followed the quarterback's eyes and cheated to his right, then took off in the direction where he thought the ball would be thrown. Rotinom, though, raced at the quarterback. A blitz wasn't called, but he was on a mission, bashing through any offensive player in his path. The quarterback aimed for a receiver who ran near the sidelines about 20 yards down, deeper from where Canton was. A defensive back was in the vicinity, but it didn't matter. As soon as the ball was thrown, Rotinom dove, his right hand clipping the ball with his fingertips, stopping what was a perfect spiral. The ball fell, and the Stormcats hollered from the bench. Gantriel sent in Joey Bexar, the second-string quarterback, to hand off the ball once and then to down it, and that was the game. Cleveland squeaked out the one-point win on the road, and stayed perfect with three wins and no losses.

In the press box, Andrews and her colleagues saw only the challenge flag, as did fans watching on television. They wouldn't know until the postgame press conference that it was Rotinom who, again, was the reason it was thrown. If there were a play of the game, that would be it.

For the media, it meant another game, another story to file about Rotinom before catching later flights.

For the players, it meant a fun, relaxing plane ride home.

For Rotinom, it meant reading time, until Doc picked him up at the airport.

CHAPTER 18

Andrews filed her dispatch from the San Jose press box, gathered her items and took a cab to the airport. Her flight was a couple of hours after the teams' charter. She had had a long day, with the time change, running around the stadium, grabbing quotes in the locker after the game, then back to the press box, filing her story and now wrestling with the dash to the airport. She loved her job but sometimes felt like a human pinball, being bounced from place to place when she was on the road. She looked forward to picking up Ginger from the kennel and being home.

But she was restless as the plane taxied. Something bugged her about the postgame press conference but she couldn't put her finger on it. No sooner than she had settled in with a mystery novel she fell asleep, dreaming about being a girl tossing a softball in her yard with her dad. She kept asking questions as they threw the ball back and forth, back and forth. Throw, set, catch. Throw, set, catch.

"Dad, how does a baseball pitcher throw a curve ball?" she asked, still wearing her softball uniform after a game.

"Why do you wanna know?" her dad asked, smiling. "Gonna start throwing one?"

"I just want to know," she said, catching the ball.

"Well," he said, as he caught her toss and moved near

her, "You hold it like this"—he used the softball to show her the basics of the grip—"and spread your index and middle finger like this across the seams. Then when you throw it, you do this" he snapped his wrist in an awkward, unnatural motion.

"That looks like it would hurt," Andrews said.

"It can, especially if you're too young to throw it," he said. "Promise me you won't try to throw one."

"OK, dad, I promise."

They backed up and kept throwing, the twilight slowly fading. Catharine's legs were caked with dirt and a bit of blood from scooping up grounders.

"Dad, why do they call a suicide squeeze in baseball a 'suicide'?" she asked.

"Always the questions," her father said, smiling. He never minded them. "Well, when a team at bat has a man on third and it wants to surprise the other team, it signals the man to steal home. But the batter has to bunt the ball—you remember that part?"

"Sure dad, I just don't get the 'suicide' part."

"Well, if the bunt is laid down and the runner gets a good jump, the run has a chance to score. But if the batter misses the bunt, then the runner is —"

"A dead duck?" Catharine asked.

Her dad smiled. "You got it."

"I guess it's kind of like a blitz in football? Like when you told me the defense has to gamble when the linebacker tries to tackle the quarterback?"

"Yes, honey, like that. They're both gambles," he said.

Catharine was quiet for a moment as she tossed the ball back. Her dad was still in his white dress shirt, slacks and loafers, though he had taken off his tie and rolled up his sleeve.

"Dad?" she asked, "If a football team has a really big guy can they let him stand under the goal posts to jump up and block a field goal? You know, like a real long one that might barely get through?"

Her dad thought for a moment. "No, I don't think so. Actually, a team might have tried that a long time ago, and I think it's outlawed now. But I'm not positive."

Catharine and her dad kept tossing the ball, but the image of a big guy jumping up and blocking field goals kept running through her mind. Suddenly Riga Rotinom was playing catch with them, but not talking. He would just catch and throw, catch and throw. Every throw was the same, right on the money to Catharine's glove. It was almost mesmerizing.

"How come you don't need a glove?" she asked. But he wouldn't answer. He would just catch and throw, never dropping the ball, never making an errant throw.

Just then a stewardess pushed through the drink cart and the rattling woke Catharine, the game of catch with her, her dad and Rotinom disappearing in an instant.

"Drink, ma'am?"

"Water, please," she said as she blinked the sleep out. As she pulled down her tray table she got out her notes and PDR and starting jotting numbers. 17+15+16 = 48. Rotinom's tackles. She calculated how many tackles he would have at the end of the season if he kept going at this rate— about 290 tackles when the season ended. Andrews didn't know the league's tackle record off the top of her head, but 290 seemed extraordinarily high. She doubted anyone was even close to half that. She emailed Sails to check on the team record, then started doodling a giant football player, batting footballs like King Kong swatting planes.

She thought back to the press conference and locker-room interviews, her restlessness coming back. Something nagged. She remembered the interviews as she huddled in the mass of reporters asking questions. It was as if something were out of place, something was there that shouldn't have been. It looked usual enough—strewn towels hanging on chairs and benches; tape ripped off and wadded, with twisted strands tailing like comets and left on the floor. The smell of sweat from the pads that clung to bodies wafted throughout the room. Players sat, tired from the hard-fought game. It was quieter than usual. It had been a tough game, each team looking for that one score to break it open, and ending in a low-scoring, defensive showdown. Gantriel gave his usual "We need to execute our offense better" quotes. Everyone was tired. Balany looked drained. Canton was fairly quiet. Rotinom was…

Suddenly, Andrews sat up, jostling her tray table. She realized what was wrong with the picture, but she didn't know why. It was Rotinom. Other than a few grass stains on his jersey and across his thigh pads, he looked fresh.

Andrews stared at the seat-back in front of her. She had talked with Rotinom right after showers in a humid locker room. She interviewed him after games, when Rotinom was surrounded by TV lights. He had played almost every defensive snap of every game this season.

Rotinom, she realized, never sweated.

CHAPTER 19

The thought nagged Catharine when the plane landed, when she got home, and when she walked Ginger. She didn't know why Rotinom didn't sweat, but she'd pay attention after Thursday's game against Houston at Emerald Lake Stadium. She fell asleep on the couch with Ginger curled at her side.

The week was a blur. A couple of Stormcats had lingering injuries she'd have to check on, and Andrews' editor asked her to speak to a grade school about her job. The fifth, sixth and seventh grades of a local school were bringing in "professionals" to speak at a career day. Catharine would explain what she did for a living. The last time she went to a career day the kids were fine but the principal wanted to talk about the Stormcats. Once she talked to kindergartners, their silent, in-awe faces staring at Catharine as she gave a short, animated talk about her job. She kept it simple, describing what she does as a storyteller which, in fact, is exactly correct. She was feeling pretty good about it. When she finished she asked "Does anyone have any questions?"

A little girl's hand shot straight up.

"Yes?" Catharine asked.

"Do you know how to make chocolate cake?"

So much for a second career in public speaking.

These kids were older, and the speech went well. The team practiced, and autumn set into Cleveland. The team's week changed a bit because of having less time to prepare for the Thursday-night kickoff. The usual players found their way to ajo to watch the Monday-night game, but some were still catching up with their sleep cycles and begged off. When Andrews drove through the city streets to wind up at the stadium Thursday afternoon, it seemed like it should be Sunday to her.

She liked the drive, except for the rah-rah kelly green stripes alongside the white lines in the middle of the road near the stadium. It took a City Council vote to alter the city street structure in any way, but Scranton invited council members three at a time to games, and eventually they unanimously passed legislation to allow the painting of the stripes. The team paid for the paint, and because Scranton talked to council members three at a time, a majority of them was never present at once. That was important, because it meant the meetings stayed private, and everything stayed behind closed doors. Should they have met together it would have constituted a public meeting, and would have gone to a vote and rules would have been in place to follow and everyone involved just figured why bother? So the neighborhood, like it or not, had kelly green stripes running alongside the white one.

She settled in to the press box and finished gathering her notes by the time Houston took the field. Cleveland kicked off, a deep boomer into the end zone.

The quarterback came out, and in the true spirit of Texas tried to go for it all on the first play. Apparently either impatience or a scouting report or a combination of both led them to believe this was a good play to call.

It wasn't.

Rotinom read it perfectly. Even Canton was caught a bit flat-footed, expecting a run right off the bat. But Rotinom shot through the line, untouched. It was a sprint to the quarterback. He bypassed the center and surged forward, slamming the quarterback into the ground, a bone-crushing blow that knocked him straight back. His helmet and the ball both popped free, causing a scramble for everyone except the motionless QB. He lay still as the chaotic scramble for the fumble moved behind him. One player kicked his helmet further in the dash to get to the ball. A Houston lineman pounced on the ball at the 12-yard line, only to have it squirt to the 8, where a Cleveland lineman clawed at it and pulled it in. The helmet became a soccer ball, rolling downfield, ignored. The ensuing finger-grabbing, bodies-digging pile soon was separated by the officials. Cleveland had the ball at the 8-yard line, fans were jumping in their seats, and the Stormcats sideline looked like a bobbing green mass. The only thing not moving was Houston's quarterback, out cold. Television started showing replays before the cart could wheel him to the locker room. It didn't take a doctor to determine the early diagnosis. Everyone watching knew he had a concussion.

Reilly Carver took a pitchout from Balany and ran it in on the Stormcats' first play, and Cleveland was on the scoreboard.

Houston never got on track with Cronpost, their second-string QB, and Cleveland rolled. Culpepper caught a touchdown pass, Thomas ran one in, and Polsky hit a late field goal to cap a 23-0 game. Balany kept getting better as the season went along. He was helped by Wisgenti and

LeBon staying healthy. The Stormcat signal-caller had a strong running game to go along with healthy receivers, and he threw for more than 200 yards.

Balany loved the game, and the game loved him. He had led the stereotypical life of a quarterback, dating a cheerleader in high school, being named all-American in college and then becoming a first-round draft choice. He had managed to protect his 6-foot, 3-inch frame from serious damage throughout his career. In his 30s, he played to win, and while he never seemed to shed the "big man on campus" persona, he played because of his passion for the game. He had aged and slowed some, but the 12-year-old stayed in him, the one who set up targets in his back yard, taking snaps from an imaginary center, fading back and throwing.

Andrews raced a little faster to the locker rooms. She had to find out more details about the injury to the Houston quarterback, but she also needed to see Rotinom. She went to Houston's lockers first.

She jotted the details of the quarterback's injury, made a note to call a doctor source of hers to ask about concussions, then ran to the Stormcats' locker room.

The humidity from the showers in the back coupled with the added bodies made it warm. Anyone wearing a sweater regretted it. Reporters were fanned throughout the room. No surprise; there were many heroes today, and Rotinom's double-digit tackle effort was getting to be expected. He had 14 more today, including the sack on the first play.

The room was thick from all the bodies and TV lights. Andrews squeezed past the equipment and microphones to the front, angling for a look at the big man. She bent like a wrestler, maneuvering for a better vantage, popped her head through and looked up at him.

He wasn't sweating.

CHAPTER 20

Brooks Scranton had a busy day ahead of him. After making sure plans were in place for the team's European jaunt, the back-to-back games against Frankfurt and London, he was zoning out, gazing across the practice field from his office, daydreaming.

The buzz from his phone broke his daydreaming. He recognized Daugava's number.

"Mr. Scranton, you are well I presume?"

"Yes, very. Your nephew is having quite a season," Scranton said, expecting the call.

"I am glad to hear. As I told you, it is difficult for me to quantify 'good' in football. I trust your opinion," the doctor said.

Scranton chuckled. "Better than good—great. He is having a tremendous impact on the field. That's actually something I wanted to talk about. He never...tires, of course, which leads me to a question."

"Yes?" Doc answered.

"Could he—doc, do you know what 'playing both ways' means in football?"

"I'm afraid I don't," Daugava said.

"It's a player who plays both offense and defense," Scranton said.

"I see. Is it common?" Daugava asked.

"No," said Scranton, chuckling to himself over the doctor's football naïveté. "As a matter of fact, it is very uncommon. Players in most sports are very specialized. Football, as you know, requires a lot of endurance. It would be too much to ask the human body to take on much more."

"The human body, yes," Daugava said. "I understand Mr. Scranton. Could he play twice as much as he is playing?"

"Yes," answered Scranton. "Essentially it would be twice as much. Very few breaks. You have worked so hard with him, he is in excellent shape, and I just wondered—"

"Yes, I do believe he could," Daugava interjected. "We have made sure he is in excellent shape."

"Excellent," Scranton repeated as he leaned back in his chair, still surveying the empty field. Then he pulled himself upright. "One more thing, Doc, in the Houston game—did you watch?"

"Yes, I did. How is the Houston player, number 14?"

"McGuinness, the quarterback," Scranton said. "He will be fine, but might miss this week's game."

"I am sorry. I will, how would you say, offer some fine-tuning advice to Riga, to maybe…play more careful?"

Scranton sighed again. "That would be fine. I don't want him to play with any less enthusiasm, I just want him to, well, not to…"

"Play with too much aggression to be penalized?" Daugava said.

"Exactly," Scranton smiled as the doctor finished his sentence once again. "You do seem like you have picked up a bit of American football knowledge. Your nephew is turning you into a fan."

"I believe he is, Mr. Scranton, I believe he is."

Scranton hung up and stared back at the field, its side-lines littered with tackling sleds, dummies and stationary bikes. He thought back to summer drills, when the offense and defenses would be broken for play after play after play. He would watch assistants and quarterbacks throw 25-yard passes down the sidelines to streaking receivers, who worked on getting their timing down. He would watch the quarterbacks, the only players in a different colored jersey, a warning that said, "don't touch me, I can't afford to get hurt in practice." He would hear the horn blare every 10 minutes or so to signal a shift in drills, or time to run sprints. He firmly believed he could sense a difference in which players ran hard and who was dogging it. Body language, he always felt, went a long way.

Several years back he had the idea to open preseason drills to the public. So he installed bleachers, set up vendor booths and charged a nominal fee—half the price going for upkeep of the field he had to pay for anyway, and half going to charity. In one quick and easy stroke, he fostered good will in the community and made a few bucks to help cover field maintenance.

Fans ate it up. Occasionally there was the fan who liked to yell "Pick it up, pick it up!" at a lineman lumbering through half-speed drills, but all in all it turned out to be a good idea.

Scranton's next call was to Gantriel. He moved to his desk and had his secretary summon the coach, who came immediately into Gantriel's office. Scranton dismissed the usual pleasantries and got down to business, knowing Gantriel had as much patience for small talk as he did.

"Coach, you know I don't meddle in your game plan, right?"

"Sure Mr. Scranton," Gantriel said. Though the two men weren't that far apart in age Gantriel always used the title when addressing the owner. "But why do I feel there's a 'but' coming in the next sentence?"

Scranton laughed. "And any owner would be crazy to muck up a system that's running smoothly."

Gantriel nodded. "Yes, sir, but I still feel that 'but' coming."

Gantriel smiled. "But…" he let the word linger as Gantriel lifted his eyebrows. "I have a suggestion. It's yours to decide; I just want to throw something out on the table."

Gantriel eyed him skeptically. "I'm listening."

"Rotinom has, well… he has excellent stamina. His personal regimen kept him in very good shape—surprisingly to me, since he never played before, but in great shape nonetheless."

"Surprising to me, too," Gantriel agreed.

"And he has proven to be pretty savvy on the field," the owner said.

Gantriel nodded again. "He is."

Scranton stood and leaned over his desk. A gold business-card holder, a cup of coffee and a rarely used desk blotter were the only items fighting for room with his cell phone and computer in the virtually paperless office. Scranton stared at Gantriel for a moment, then blurted out his thought: "Would you consider playing him both ways, using him on the offensive line?"

Gantriel looked up. "Play both ways? With the game what it is today?" The coach stared at Scranton.

"It's your decision, entirely," Scranton said. "I just, well, I noticed his stamina on the field late in the game and thought it might be worth throwing out there. He learned the defense on a pretty steep learning curve."

The men shared a moment of silence as the coach let sink in what the owner had just suggested.

"That would be…" Gantriel let his thought drift off, but Scranton knew what the coach was thinking.

"A game changer," he said.

Gantriel nodded. He wasn't one to hog glory. "It's a good idea. I'll talk to him about it, get him with other linemen, have him read up on the offensive plays. He seems to read quite a bit, I hear."

"Yes, he does," Scranton said. "He reads, and he remembers."

Gantriel was lost in his thoughts. If Rotinom could play both sides of the ball, his impact would be amazing. He already was a one-man force on defense. Putting him on offense would change everything.

Gantriel stood to face his owner. "I'll speak with him, let him study the book in Europe," he said, and walked out across the plush rug, leaving a smiling Scranton whose day-dreams had turned from the practice field to the thoughts of his team's success. They were undefeated, and Scranton started to believe they would stay that way.

He thought back to when he was a child and remembered his family's tradition of cutting down a tree for Christmas. One year, as he was waiting for his father to choose the tree to be cut and hoisted on the family car, he watched as two workers wrestled with a tree, trying to shove it into a twine-wrapping machine. They fed the tree into the machine, which shredded branches as it encircled it in twine. It could swallow a tree, which would corkscrew its way into and out of the machine, leaving it like a mummy wrapped in brown rope. Except when one of the workers pushed the tree, a branch caught his hat and yanked it off his head. The hat snagged on a branch and went in the chipping side of the machine, which didn't care about what was fed in. It grabbed and tore anything in its path with its internal claws. The tree came out, wrapped tightly and neatly, and the hat was spit out in pieces, shreds of yellow and black shot out all over the snow.

Scranton hadn't thought of that image in years.

CHAPTER 21

While players slept or listened to music on the flight to Frankfurt, Rotinom sat the entire time, reading the playbook. The Xs and Os would look Greek to a novice, but Rotinom seemed to have an intuitive sense to figuring it all out. Balany and several linemen offered their help to go over plays, but so far, Rotinom hadn't asked. He had calmly taken the assignment to play both sides of the ball from Gantriel, and now set to studying.

Each player had one seat to himself, with a small aisle separating him from a teammate. So everyone had, in effect, a window seat that also was an aisle seat. LeBon sat across from Thomas.

"… So what did the dealer say when you told them you liked the car?"

"Well, he asked me how much I was willing to pay. So I told him twenty bucks," Thomas said.

"What did he do?" LeBon asked.

"He said, 'No, really, how much do you want to pay for the car?' I told him again—'twenty dollars.'"

LeBon smiled and tipped back iced tea.

"So this goes on, you see, and he asks me again. You know I can be a bit stubborn, right?"

LeBon smiled. "You? Nah."

Thomas ignored the sarcasm and kept the story going.

"So I tell him again. He keeps asking, I keep answering. Finally he gets the sales manager. Guy comes over and what does he ask me?"

"How much do you wanna pay for the car?" LeBon guessed.

"Right. So I tell him the same thing. And what does he do? He starts off with the same response as the sales guy—how much do you really want to pay blah blah blah."

"So what do you say?" LeBon asked.

"I tell him, 'When you fellas decide when you want to tell me how much you are willing to sell me the damn car, we can talk. I already told you how much I am willing to pay for it.' And I start to walk out. Now they're both going crazy. But I walked out."

"And?" LeBon asked.

"And I went down the street to another dealer, and when he started in with 'how much do you wanna pay' I said, 'twenty dollars' and stared at him. He said 'Well, I'd hate to sell you this car for twenty dollars 'cause I would lose my shirt, and my pants, and my job, and they would lock me up in a nuthouse for selling a car then I wouldn't be able to keep my house or my dog, and I really love that dog. But that's not the worst part.' So now he's got me going. So I ask him, 'What's the worst part?' And he says, 'Losing my Stormcat season tickets and not getting Bronx Thomas into one of my cars.' "

LeBon smiled. "Get out."

"No, man, really. I get a shaggy-dog story from this guy and he ends with that. So he knows who I am, says he played fullback in high school, and we get the deal done inside of 15 minutes."

"Hey you think I could go to this guy? I need new wheels," LeBon said.

"Nah," Thomas said. "He said he hates receivers."

Several rows up Carver and Balany sat, a row behind Culpepper and McAdams.

"Carver, word man, give it to us," Culpepper said, leaning forward.

"Word of the day, gents, is 'MacGuffin,'" said Carver, looking up from his crossword puzzle.

"Mahguffwhat?" said McAdams, his hulking frame looking uncomfortable crammed even in an oversized airline seat. Everything about McAdams was big, even his fingers, sausage links poking from his hand. When he was a kid his nickname was "Husky."

Balany looked up. "Yeah, that's a new one to me, too."

"MacGuffin," Carver repeated. "Means something in a story, you know, like a thing or a person, that acts as a device to keep the plot moving along, except the thing or person isn't really all that important."

"Ah," said Balany.

"MacGuffin," repeated McAdams. "I thought that was the Houston quarterback who Rotinom almost killed."

Canton turned back from his seat. "That was McGuinness," he said. "You should always know the name of the guy you plant on the field."

Players laughed. "Where is Rotinom?" someone asked.

"Back in the loud seat," Canton said, referring to the seat next to the bathrooms, one that most of the players avoided. "Said he needed to read. Man is going to play both ways, gentlemen."

"Man is crazy," said Culpepper.

"Not as crazy as Polsky," McAdams said about the Stormcats' kicker. "Guy says he likes soccer, gonna try to catch a game or two on this trip."

"What's so crazy about watching soccer?" someone asked.

"Because the game is 300 miles from our stadium," McAdams said. "He's gonna rent a car and go. Doesn't speak German."

"That true Polsky?" someone asked.

The kicker, a few rows back, leaned forward. "Yeah, it's a solid sport."

"But driving 300 miles?" someone asked.

Before Polsky replied Wisgenti chipped in. "I think," he said, "every time a kicker misses a game-winning field goal, you should have a finger chopped off."

"Aww man," Polsky said as the players laughed again. "You know what I think? I think lineman who miss a block should have their—"

The pilot's voice cut him off, announcing the plane's approach. The plane touched down in Germany, and on the concourse Francis caught up with Rotinom.

"You get much studying done? What do you think of the plays?"

Rotinom turned toward Francis and paused for a second.

"I remember them," he said.

Francis stopped him for a moment. "What do you mean 'I remember them'? You memorized the entire playbook on one five-hour flight?"

"No," Rotinom said. "Read playbook in preseason and at home. Read playbook again on plane."

"That's impossible," Francis said. "There are hundreds of plays, even more looks, variations. How could you possibly—"

"I remember them all," Rotinom said, and kept on walking, leaving Francis standing, staring, in the concourse.

CHAPTER 22

When the offense lined up at Stadion Frankfurt, there was one unhappy face on the sidelines, and it wasn't for lack of sleep because of the change of time zones. It was Lanier Broda, the center who had lost his starting job because the coaches decided Rotinom would play both ways, at least in the first quarter. Broda used to be famous for wearing size 22 cleats and being a decent center. With Rotinom in the lineup, people went back to talking about his big feet.

Sails had sprung the news on the media in his pregame notes, and Andrews and Trent and the rest of their colleagues all had the same questions running through their heads for Gantriel: Why now? How is he able? Did he want to or was he asked? What's his conditioning like? How can a rookie be expected to remember the plays? The postgame press conference promised to be a fun one.

The Stormcats took the opening kickoff and started at their own 19. And sure enough, walking out with the offense into the huddle was Rotinom, looking like that one kid on the first day of eighth grade who had seen a growth spurt over summer and towered among his peers.

"All right boys, let's get it going," Balany said in the huddle, glancing at the fresh faces around him.

"Six option shoot with fire, on three—that's six option shoot with fire on three, ready break!"

The offense clapped hands—a crisp sound that by game's end would be a dull, tired thud, its sharp clap lost to exhaustion, tape and dirt.

Balany strode to the line behind the big man, feeling a sense of protection, and called the play.

"Red! Forty-two! Forty-two! Hut, hut, HUT!" Balany shouted, the colors and numbers not meaning anything at this point. Rotinom snapped the ball on cue and surged into the man in front of him, knocking him backward with little effort. But instead of staying down, Rotinom pushed himself back up quickly and swung to his right, where Carver was running. Balany's call was a fake handoff to Thomas—that's what the "with fire" indicated in the play—and a quick pitch to Carver. The "six" signified which hole in the line Carver should target; a gap between two linemen on the right should open, if everyone hit their blocking assignments.

Rotinom knew the play. He swung to his right in front of Carver and blocked away a defender as the running back juked a linebacker coming at him, then raced for 13 yards.

"Good start, boys, good start," Balany said.

Carver tapped Rotinom's helmet as they regrouped in the huddle. "Nice block big man, nice to have you on the right side of the ball."

"You see that noseguard?" someone said. "Guy got driven all the way to Berlin."

Chuckles all around until Balany quieted them and called the next play.

Second down started like first down.

Rotinom snapped the ball, Balany faked to Thomas, and the noseguard was driven back, landing on his seat.

This time, though, Balany had another option, and he took it. Gantriel had installed passing plays earlier than usual in his game plan, trying to exploit the Frankfurt defensive backs, and Balany looked deep. Wisgenti beat his man, caught the pass in stride, and went in untouched. Sixty-eight yards for six points. The two-point conversion call was a no-brainer; Balany took the snap and practically walked in behind Rotinom.

And when the defense lumbered onto the field, Rotinom was right there, his only break being the trot to the sidelines to watch the kickoff.

And then it was the Rotinom-Canton show. Rotinom rushing, pressuring the quarterback, causing problems. Canton found his way to the ball on almost every play, the determination and heart he had for football shining through. Rotinom flushed out the quarterback, who seemed to be running a little scared after seeing the many replays of what happened to McGuinness in the Houston game. On a third-down play late in the first quarter, Rotinom blitzed, and half the line seemed to capsize on him to slow him down. But Canton read the play right, and had cheated to his right. He accelerated, leaped, and intercepted the pass. He stumbled for a few yards before being hit by two Frankfurt linemen.

Cleveland's bench went crazy as the defense swarmed around Canton, who jogged to the sidelines, still holding the treasured ball. He finally flipped it to a referee, then looked around for Rotinom as the coaches and players gathered on the sidelines.

At least one photographer would capture the image of the solitary Rotinom, standing near where the ball would be placed. The giant player's arms rested on his waist as he waited for his offensive colleagues to take the field. Some tape had unraveled from his wrist, but otherwise he looked fresh. He had figured out quickly it was wasted effort to jog to the sidelines only to have to turn around.

In the press box, incredulous reporters sat, stunned. Sails' staff worked on the play-by-play account they would give to the press after each quarter. Rotinom's name would be on virtually every line.

On the Cleveland sidelines, Francis looked at Gantriel the way he did the first time they saw Rotinom play. Gantriel looked up and saw Rotinom waiting, patiently. The coach shook his head, barely believing what he had seen from this one player.

And on the Frankfurt sidelines, the defensive coordinator berated his noseguard, whose forehead had a cut with blood dripping down the bridge of his nose. He was breathing hard, trying to catch his breath. He looked as if he had played a full game instead of just a few plays.

Again, Cleveland cruised to a win. With an early lead, Balany called fake after fake, and the Frankfurt defense—not wanting to be burned again—kept a watchful eye on the receivers. It didn't matter. It was Carver off-tackle, Carver running wide. He shoulder-faked his way, turning a 4-yard gain into 7. He scampered around linemen and turned on the jets. He converted short passes into longer gains. He was like a basketball player, a shooter with a hot hand. When it was over he had accounted for 213 all-purpose yards—168 rushing, and 45 receiving.

In the end, it was 31-3, and even Gantriel was cracking a smile, sort of. At 5-0 and atop their division, he could afford to. Scranton, who had made the trip, watched from a private box as he scanned lines on the play-by-play sheets.

9:36 Carver 8 gain right side Rotinom block
8:45 Thomas 4 gain middle Rotinom block
8:16 Balany pass incomplete, Wisgenti intended
7:28 Frankft RB #35 stop at scrimmage, Rotinom tackle
6:48 Frankft QB #12 pass batted, Rotinom
And so on.

No matter when, and no matter what side of the ball, Rotinom was in on every play.

In the postgame press conference a reporter jokingly asked, to laughter, if Rotinom soon would begin playing on special teams, too. Gantriel gave his usual non-answer out of habit. But as Scranton watched in his box via closed-circuit coverage, he wondered if that wouldn't be a bad idea.

CHAPTER 23

Rotinom's presence on offense helped open more holes for Carver, but it was Balany who was really clicking. He steadied the troops, coordinating drives and keeping the Stormcats focused on the field.

Cleveland followed the Frankfurt win the following Sunday with a 24-7 victory against London in a new stadium, converted from an old club soccer field into an all-purpose athletic facility. Balany threw for 285 yards, scoring on a 50-yard pass to LeBon. Carver ran one in from the 8-yard line, and Culpepper grabbed one from 13 yards out, leaping in the back of the end zone and pulling down the ball as a defender pushed him out of bounds. Two-point conversions were becoming automatic with Rotinom on the line; everyone in the stadium knew the call would be a quarterback sneak up the middle, but there was little the London defense could do. If defenders capsized around Rotinom, Balany could roll and throw. But usually it was Rotinom driving a hole through the defense the way a power drill pushes through plaster. All Balany had to do was play "follow the leader."

And through it all, Andrews watched with a nagging feeling. The team was 6-0, playing as close to perfect football on both sides of the ball as a team could play. Everything seemed to be clicking. Yet something bothered her—it wasn't a sense of doom, just a slight feeling—like something was out of order.

She had a few days off when she returned to Cleveland. After spending time with Ginger, running errands and taking care of the bills that had accumulated in her in box during her absence, she took a walk to clear her head. She came home to make a huge bowl of pasta, aimlessly chopping garlic and basil and parmesan cheese, Ginger at her side. She sipped Chianti as they settled in to watch an old movie, but jetlag caught her quickly, and she fell asleep on her couch with Ginger splayed on the floor, exhausted from begging for spaghetti strands.

Andrews' subconscious must have been working in overdrive as she slept. Because when she woke, she had a clear plan. She needed to do more to track Rotinom. Something or someone had to be out there to explain this guy. Because it really started to seem like he just materialized out of thin air, and Andrews knew that wasn't possible.

She checked and rechecked every data base she knew. She called a U.S. immigration office, seeing if they had any records on a Riga Rotinom coming to this country within the past couple of years—nothing. She checked professional license groups and found he was not a registered website owner—no surprises there, but worth checking. No speeding tickets. No tax liens. No court appearances. Not a major surprise but still worth checking.

She even grabbed at a long shot, seeing if his name was listed as a patent holder with the U.S. Patents office. Again, nothing. It seemed there wasn't one public record anywhere that had Riga Rotinom's name on it. He didn't vote, didn't drive, didn't own any property. Was never convicted of a crime, had never sued or been sued. Nothing.

Andrews took Ginger for a walk and pondered her situation. Since she couldn't get anything from the front door, she would try a back door—again: Daugava.

She remembered Daugava said he was a retired engineer. Maybe she could track down his old firm. But engineers could work anywhere.

"Wait a minute," she said suddenly, Ginger looking up on her leash. "He said 'electrical'—that has to narrow it some." Ginger looked puzzled, her brown muzz furrowed. When they got home, she went through her notebooks until she found the one from her interview in the restaurant with Daugava. She found her scrawled notes: engineer—elec— buyout. That was the clue—buyout. She sat at her computer and raced through archives of news stories. She needed a list of companies that would have employed electrical engineers. Maybe, if it were large enough, the company's buyouts would have been a news story. She couldn't remember any, but she wasn't a regular reader of business pages. Her archive system revealed 23 companies that had offered buyouts in the past 10 years and who might employ engineers. She searched an electronic phone book and looked up the first one. AIM Design, based downtown. She thought for a moment, got her spiel down, and dialed.

"AIM Design, may I help you?" a pleasant voice said.

"Hi, my name is Catharine Andrews. I am trying to locate a former employee named Janis Daugava—he took the buyout a few years ago and I need to get ahold of him."

"Let me transfer you to HR, hold please."

She listened to a radio news report before a woman picked up and she went through the introduction again. She figured she could start asking directly for HR after this.

"What was that name again?"

"Janis—J-a-n-i-s, Daugava—D-a-u-g-a-v-a." Catharine figured she better get used to spelling out the name.

"Let me guess—you're from an insurance company," the woman said as Andrews heard her typing.

"No ma'am, I am a reporter—doing a feature story on Dr. Daugava's nephew, and trying to verify some information." What Andrews wanted was to get ahold of a former colleague of Daugava's who could talk more about him. It was a far away back door, but she felt she had to get a foot in somewhere. Rotinom didn't talk, and Daugava, while pleasant, wasn't going to tell her…tell her what? She felt like she had to hunt for something but wasn't sure exactly what she was seeking. The woman said they had no record of a Janis Daugava, Andrews thanked her, hung up, and looked up the next company on the list.

No luck there, or the next, or the one after that. She kept calling, striking out, finding another company name, and calling some more.

She got down to the 22nd name out of 23, her discouragement almost as strong as her hunger. Ginger lay by her feet as she made yet another call.

"Hold please," a man said, and Andrews remained quiet.

"Yes, Daugava, he left three years ago on the buyout."

Andrews' slumped posture suddenly stiffened. Ginger even perked up. "Oh, he did, that's—thank you. Left three years ago you say?"

"Yes," said the man. "Worked in our actuation division. I'm sorry, I can't tell you where he lives, we can only give out the —"

"That's OK, I understand," Andrews said, hardly believing she had confirmed what she needed on the second-to-last company on her list. "You said 'actuation'—what do you guys do?"

"You know," he said. "Automated machinery. Big ones maneuver items in warehouses, the small ones can be used in surgeries," the man said.

"No kidding," said Andrews. "That's, uh, pretty neat." She actually did think it unique. "I didn't realize there was a company doing that in Cleveland, and I have lived here for years."

Andrews thanked the man for his time, and then looked up more information on the company. Zadrandall Automation was based not far from where the doctor lives, she figured, in an older part of Cleveland. Funny, she thought, a modern company in an old part of town.

Andrews checked her watch as her stomach rumbled. Almost 5 o'clock. She threw on an old sweater and tennis shoes, grabbed a smaller notebook so she didn't look like Jane Reporter, dumped food into Ginger's dish, and left.

Like many reporters, Andrews kept her car stocked with old maps and phone books, even though her PDR included computerized maps that could be called up instantly. She had to find a colleague, someone who knew the doctor. While she knew the general area where she was going, she needed something specific, a comfortable place that served food and drink and was near the company's plant.

As Andrews drove, she figured a plan of attack. What she wanted was to talk to someone who might know something, anything, about Daugava. What she was figuring was engineers are like anyone else, and they might want to relax someplace before heading home. And hopefully, Andrews thought, the place would serve food. Good food.

CHAPTER 24

Andrews found Zadrandall Automation easily enough, but slowed to cruise the area, looking for a gathering spot, a restaurant, anything. She found a couple of old shops, a hardware / fix-it store that had stayed in business because the larger big-box stores rarely ventured into older, city neighborhoods. Most had turned into online clearing-houses anyway. A gift shop and a hair salon sandwiched a drugstore. Leaves scattered across the small sidewalk as Andrews glanced at placards for fund-raisers in the shops' windows. She was about to turn on a side street when she saw a light. She looked up to see "Mary-Jo's Grill" at the end of the block. Andrews pulled in front and saw the smaller-print "Best cheeseburgers in town" sign amid the neon signs hanging in the window. Her stomach grumbled and she made her way in.

Clattering pool balls sounded as she approached the long bar on her right. A woman wiped the area in front of Andrews and asked what she wanted.

"Cheeseburgers really the best in town?" Andrews asked the woman, who was older than she was and looked a bit tired.

"Ahh, a first-timer," she said. "You bet—made to order."

"You know," Andrews said, "I'm parched and starving—

I'll have a big glass of water and one of those famous cheeseburgers, well done, and with a side of fries."

"You got it," the woman said and disappeared.

Andrews looked around. Half a dozen pool tables were to the left of the bar. A television perched over each corner. The dark green curtain that hung along the front window looked like it hadn't been washed in years, its bottoms frayed and dingy. Probably from the grease from the best cheeseburgers in town, Andrews thought. A Stormcats poster with the season schedule was stuck on a patch of wall.

The woman reappeared and topped off her water glass. Most of the people in the bar were middle-aged men in ties.

"Pool helps them relax," the woman said.

"Who?" Andrews asked.

The woman nodded to the tables. "Them. The techies, the engineers. Most of 'em work at Zadrandall down the street. They're not bad pool players, either. Helps them unwind after a day at the plant, I guess. I've been here almost as long as that plant, and I still don't know exactly what they do there."

Andrews looked up from her water. "They build automated machinery," she said, catching the woman's surprise look. "Mechanics that move around boxes in warehouses, for instance. Smaller ones for surgeries." In a few seconds Andrews gave her all the recent knowledge she had acquired and sounded like she knew what she was talking about.

"No kidding?" the woman said. "What brings you here—you don't look like the engineer type."

"Girls can't be engineers?" Catharine said.

"Hehh, not at that plant, apparently. I rarely see women come in here."

Andrews smiled. "Actually I know someone who used to work at the plant, and I was trying to find some information on him."

"Ahh," said the woman. "Say no more, I got it. Checking out a boyfriend."

"Well, no, not exactly," Andrews said. "More like I'm a reporter and want to see if this guy was being straight with me. He's nice enough—I mean, I just need to verify his story." The woman eyed Andrews with a slightly suspicious nod. "Who are you a reporter for?"

"The American," Andrews said.

"Oh, the sports paper, got it," she said. Andrews knew the answer to that question was an important one; if the person she was talking to didn't like her employer for any reason, well, conversations could sometimes end abruptly.

Once she interviewed a guy who took out his frustration of seeing too many typos in The American by getting upset with Andrews, who tried to explain she tried to avoid typos. He wouldn't have it, though, and wouldn't talk to Andrews. But this woman seemed different.

"I'm Catharine Andrews," she said, offering a hand.

"I'm Mary-Jo," the woman said, flinging a rag over one shoulder and taking Andrews' hand.

"Ah," she said, "The Mary-Jo herself."

"In the flesh. Inherited this place 20 years ago from my dad."

"Funny," Andrews said, "I've been in the city for years but I don't think I came across this bar before. And it's the kind of place I like."

"You like pool joints with engineers?" Mary-Jo asked as she brought out an odd-looking, multi-pronged holder of condiments. Each compartment held pickles, salt and pepper, a ketchup bottle, mustard container and squeeze bottle of salsa.

"No," Andrews said, "I like quiet places with good cheeseburgers."

"Well, that we have," Mary-Jo said, walking to the end of the bar to tend to a customer. Andrews sipped her water and watched two men at a nearby table. One was lining up a tough shot—the cue sat a couple of inches from the two-ball. He had to hit the cue ball the length of the table, off the far rail, then hope for it to bounce all the way back, knocking the two into the corner pocket. His opponent watched as the man crouched, took careful aim, and shot. The white ball traveled the length of the table, bounced off the rail and slowly rolled toward the two-ball. It missed and just kept rolling, finally resting against the rail.

"Tough shot," said the other man, who circled the table for his turn. When Andrews turned back around Mary-Jo was there with a plate holding a large cheeseburger, its oozing grease and dripping cheese encroaching on the fries.

"Enjoy," she said.

"Thanks," said Andrews, who momentarily forgot why she was there as she sank her teeth into the burger, wanting to taste it before adjusting it with condiments. Maybe it was because she was starving, but Andrews thought she might have been wrong to doubt the "Best cheeseburgers in town" claim.

Mary-Jo reappeared to see a chomping Andrews.

"OK," Andrews said between bites. "What's the secret? When I cook this at home it comes out like a dry patty that might resemble a burger, if I'm lucky."

"The old grill," Mary-Jo said, smiling, as she turned on the TVs to a sportscast, despite the fact that few were paying attention to anything but their pool games. "I don't use the new grills that cook meat in a few seconds. I bought one of them old ones, the way they used to grill 'em up years ago. Takes a few minutes and is a bear to clean, but well worth it."

"I haven't eaten anything cooked on the old grills in years. They came out with all those cancer studies. I thought they outlawed them."

"Well, let's just say I found a legal loophole to be grandfathered in."

Andrews raised her eyebrows but was too busy chewing to inquire further. But Mary-Joe continued.

"I found some wording on the city books that allowed me to bring in an older grill. Kind of a technicality. You know the difference between a good technicality and a bad one?" she said.

"Nope," Catharine said between bites.

"If it works for you, it's a good one."

Catharine smiled.

"I'm used to the instant stove tops," Andrews said.

"Most people are," Mary-Jo said, "and they're missing out. Yeah I know, it's not as healthy and all that, but it's damn good."

Andrews nodded in agreement as she swallowed another bite. "Hey," she said, "about this guy I came in to find out about. Do you know anyone in here who's been at the plant a while who might know him? He left several years ago."

Mary-Jo surveyed her patrons and spotted one at the end of the bar, zoning out on the television above him. "Try him," she said, nodding in his direction. "Comes in here regularly. I don't know him real well, but he works at Zadrandall. Don't know what he does but he might have an idea."

"Thanks," said Andrews, who turned her attention back to what was becoming the most important task of the night, finishing the best cheeseburger in town.

When the final fry was dipped in the final dab of mustard, Andrews wiped her hands on her napkins and took her water glass down to the end of the bar, where the man was still staring at the TV as he circled the glass in front of him with his index finger.

"Excuse me, sir, I was wondering if I could ask you something, my name is Catharine Andrews, I work for—"

"Hi," the man interrupted. "Name's Ed. Mary-Jo came down here a little while ago and told me you were trying to find someone. I didn't bother you because you were engrossed in the burger."

Andrews smiled. "That was my first cheeseburger here," she said, "and it WAS good."

"Like the sign says," Ed said. "So who's the guy?"

"His name is Daugava, Janis Daugava. He used to work in the—"

"Actuation, sure I know him—haven't seen him for years, though, since he left. What's he done?"

"Actually, nothing," Andrews said. "I just needed to verify he was on the level when he said he worked as an engineer."

"Yes, he worked with me on some projects over the years. Nice enough guy but kept to himself. Was one of those guys who did his job and went home, and really didn't share his home life. Least that's the way I figured him."

"What exactly does Zadrandall Automation do?" Andrews asked. "I mean, I know about the machinery for surgeries and warehouses, but I keep picturing a big place full of these machines being tested."

"Actually, it's a two-pronged operation. The top brass is really a sales force—they sell the stuff guys like me make. Basically, teams of mostly electrical and mechanical engineers work together on various projects, working to get the kinks out until, well, all the kinks are out."

"How long does that take? Sounds like a lot of work. How do you know when it's done?" Andrews asked.

"That's the simple part," Ed said. "It's done when a guy goes into a room and hits a remote-control lever, and the machine does what it's supposed to do, as many times as the guy wants a task done."

"You mean, you hit 'left' and it goes left, you hit 'right' and it goes right, and that's it?" Andrews asked.

"Well, the commands can be—and are continuing to be—more and more specific. But that's essentially it."

"And Janis worked with you?"

"Sometimes. He was quite good. Most of us have specialties—electrical, for instance. The teams are created to match up all areas of expertise. Janis was one of the few guys who could fill in almost any role on the teams."

"Did he work on the industrial arms, the ones for warehouses, or the small ones for surgeries?" Andrews asked.

"Mostly the larger ones. Which are smaller, in a way."

"What do you mean?" Catharine asked, confused.

"Well, the larger ones have a lot more wires in them, but… well, it's kind of hard to explain. There's a lot of moving pieces. If you're on the larger ones there's a lot of smaller components you have to keep track of. But like I said, he was versatile. I think he could have been a manager here, but he always turned down promotions, saying he liked his work and didn't want to become a 'paper pusher,' as he used to say. That's what he called the managers."

"And you use the big ones to move stuff around in a warehouse?"

"That's a big part of it. With all the big-box stores going online in the last few years, they turned their stores into mailing centers, but some of what they sell are pretty heavy. Makes more sense to have an adjustable arm to grab, say, a box of 10 bicycles and shift them where they need to be, rather than having someone do it one by one."

"Makes sense," Andrews said.

"I tell you," Ed continued, "the guy really liked his job."

"Was he sad to leave, with the buyout and all?"

Ed thought for a moment. "You know, I don't think so. He seemed happy. But to tell you the truth, I don't remember much about him personally. He took all his lunch breaks alone. Occasionally we would have a cup of coffee, but he always ate by himself, and I don't think he ever came here. I think someone once said he had an elderly mother from the old country he looked after, but I really don't know."

"I know he's from Latvia originally," Andrews said.

"That's right," Ed said, "but he never even talked about that. I don't even know how long he was in this country or if he came here to study or for the job or what."

"About the only thing I know about Latvia is that it's about the size of West Virginia," Andrews said.

Mary-Jo sauntered over and asked if anyone needed a drink. Ed looked at his glass, a splash of whiskey left over the remnants of ice. "Put his on my tab," Andrews said, "and I'll have another water."

"And the burger?" Mary-Jo asked.

"Your sign is accurate," Andrews replied.

Mary-Jo smiled and walked away. Andrews swirled her bar stool back toward Ed, who had on an old tan corduroy sports coat, white shirt, blue tie and tan pants. His loafers were a bit scuffed and his shirt somewhat wrinkled. Andrews pictured a scientist hunched over for hours putting wires together, and not really caring too much about personal style. It was a uniform that had been used by engineers for years.

"What you do? It sounds very science-fiction oriented," Andrews said.

"Well, simply put, robotic arms used in warehouses often package materials on their own, or move items from one area to another. They have been around for years. Building them is a complex project. They have to be kept clean of any dirt or grease. They have to be built to do more than lift and move, depending on the job. Our sales guys find companies who want to buy them. Guys like me make them."

Andrews swirled her water, playing a very short game of her own brand of hockey with her straw and lemon wedge.

"You look to be in deep thought," Ed said, "or maybe you are just having second thoughts on that cheeseburger."

Andrews chuckled. "No, it's interesting. I just, well, I was never much of a math or science student, so it's pretty heady stuff. I'm not the most technical person."

"Yeah, it can add up to a lot, and does," Ed said. "How did you meet Janis anyway?"

"His nephew plays for the Stormcats. I cover the team," Andrews said, still maneuvering her lemon wedge.

"No kidding? Well, like I said, I never knew anything about his family or home life. Never figured him to be much of a sports fan, he was such a quiet bookworm. Intense, in a way."

"What do you mean?" Andrews asked.

"Well, look around. Guys come here to unwind and get away from the job—a job they love and work hours concentrating on. It seemed like Janis never did anything but his job. I could be wrong, but I remember even on his lunch breaks he was reading books or writing in a notebook. Guy was constantly studying, always trying to improve himself, I guess."

Andrews was quiet for a moment as a quick daydream danced through her head. She imagined lab-coated scientists standing behind a glass-enclosed studio flipping switches as giant boxes were grabbed and moved all over the place. Then she stopped pushing her lemon wedge and thanked Ed for his time.

"You find out everything you need?" he asked.

"Well, I think so," said Andrews, who gathered her purse and swiveled the chair to face the door. "I think so."

The truth was, Catharine had some background, but nothing more. She still felt she was missing something.

CHAPTER 25

Sanangeles, the league's newest member, was next up for Cleveland. San Diego and Los Angeles had grown so much over the years, they finally blended, officially. The population was enough to support yet another team in the area. Commutes had been extended to three-plus hours each way, if someone were in a job that didn't allow telecommuting. Many folks took CalSpar—short for California Speed Rail, a lightning-quick bullet train that could zip people between San Diego and Los Angeles in 30 minutes. Andrews was glad she wasn't traveling this week. After the trip to Europe she enjoyed being home.

Sanangeles brought a 6-0 mark into Cleveland. Gantriel's challenge was to motivate his already confident players to face a solid team that had one of the best all-purpose running backs. Bobby Joe Charpnax, a kid raised amid the oil fields of west Texas, could run and catch. He could never sit still. He said he never had the moves a lot of other backs had, so he liked to lower his head and pound the defender, legs always churning, never quitting. When he was taken out of games late with the lead in hand, he wore a cream-colored cowboy hat and bounced in place with seemingly boundless energy to burn.

Coaches knew he was the guy to stop. But Gantriel

wasn't any coach. He decided early on, when he gathered with his assistants, that nothing would be changed to key in on Charpnax.

"The 5-2's been working well," he said of the Stormcats' defensive scheme that allowed for two linebackers. "You know the saying: 'If it ain't broken, don't fix it.'"

None of the coaches could, or would, argue. They were, after all, 6-0 with the best linebacker corps in the league.

Canton crouched on a bench in front of his locker, tying his shoes as he turned to look at the big man.

"99, you up for this one?"

Rotinom stared.

"You ready?" Canton repeated.

"Always," Rotinom said in the now common serious monotone.

"All right, all right," Canton said. "32's nothing, right? Just another jersey for us to stop, eh?"

"Stopping 32, no problem," came Rotinom's reply.

Canton breathed a smile even though Rotinom looked as serious as someone carefully defusing a bomb. "That's it, no problem."

Of anyone on the team, Canton had the longest, most in-depth conversations with Rotinom. The unofficial record was 10 seconds.

A slight warm front moved in late afternoon Sunday. Despite the fact Halloween was nearing, a warm breeze blew across Emerald Lake Stadium. Fans wore sweatshirts, but many didn't bother with jackets as they basked in the weather, as well as their team's success. The hype continued, the fans embraced the team, and Scranton loved it. Success on the field meant fans in the seats, merchandise sold, and money in his pocket, ultimately. Sales of Rotinom's jersey already topped a team record, and Balany's was doing well, too. On paper, Scranton was fine. All he needed was the championship.

It's all anyone on the Stormcats wanted. Or anyone in Cleveland, for that matter. Balany led his charges, having no fear, as Cleveland's offense took the field against Sanangeles. The Stormcats quickly took their opponents off-guard as Balany rolled right on first down and threw to Culpepper, a rare opening-play call for Gantriel. It was Balany's idea, and it worked. His coach might be a stern task-master most of the time, but he listened to his players. He believed in them, and they in him. Next up was Carver, who danced his way 8 yards off-tackle for the first down, and then some. Then it was Thomas through the middle for 5 more. On the next series, Balany went to the air again, hitting Wisgenti twice over the middle and Thomas in the flat. Balany ended up with the first touchdown of the day as he stood, with all the protection in the world behind his seven-four center, and found Culpepper in the corner of the end zone.

But the real treat for the fans was the vaunted matchup of Bobby Joe and the Stormcats' defense. Scranton had invited the doctor to watch with him privately in his suite, explaining the test involved for Rotinom and the defense against No. 32.

They looked from their comfortable 50-yard perch as Rotinom once again stayed on the field as his defensive mates joined him, Canton touching his arm in a quick moment of solidarity as the rest of the team gathered.

They huddled briefly, then lined up. The Sanangeles quarterback wasted no time in giving the ball to Charpnax, who sliced through the line and quickly cut to his right, looking for more. But Rotinom and Canton were on him in a shot, and down he went after a gain of 4 yards. He bounced up faster than either linebacker, saying "Boys, you got to bring it today, I feel like runnin.' " Like his legs, Bobby Joe's mouth rarely stopped.

On the next play it was a pitchout to Bobby Joe, who scampered out of bounds with some solid blocking. Third down and 2, and Rotinom and Canton both knew what was coming. They cheated in just a bit, but Canton was more cautious. They banked on the run, but if the Sanangeles quarterback threw over the middle instead, the area they were supposed to cover would be wide open. Another gamble. They inched forward, gaining a little more ground. It was as far as Canton wanted to go. Then Rotinom turned to face Canton, who caught his eye. The big man quietly said one word: "Blitz."

Canton looked at him. "Wha- what? They go run on this, they pitch wide to 32!" he half-whispered to his linebacker mate.

Rotinom repeated calmly: "Blitz."

The Sanangeles offense trudged to the line of scrimmage, as Canton saw the receivers move wide, close to the sidelines. That didn't necessarily mean pass, but he had no time to think. He made his decision; he flashed a signal behind his back to the cornerbacks that he and Rotinom would blitz—an odd call on third-and-2.

They inched even closer, and on the second "hut!" Rotinom took off, sprinting into the line. The snap came on the third "hut!" a pitch to the right to Charpnax. Rotinom shot through the line, forcing Charpnax to sidestep and change his direction. That was a mistake, because when he moved left he had no blockers, and Canton was right there. He slammed Charpnax, his legs and arms and torso hitting him in one devouring motion. The only move the running back could make was straight back and down, into the grass.

Canton's teammates surrounded him as the punting unit came on, escorting him to the sidelines where he was met with more smiles. The coaches congratulated him, not minding the gamble to blitz.

"Rotinom called it," Canton said. "He read it perfectly." Coaches looked around and spotted Rotinom staring at the field, no emotion as the Sanangeles punter prepared for the ball. He wasn't even breathing hard. And before anyone could say anything to him, he was lining up on offense.

The Stormcats again ramped to a win. They made Sanangeles resemble just another young expansion squad rather than the undefeated team they were. When the final score flashed on the giant board—33-0—it was more than a win. It left Cleveland as the sole undefeated team in the league. Bobby Joe Charpnax finished with 38 yards rushing and left with a slight concussion in the third quarter. By then, he wasn't talking much.

Scranton and Daugava relaxed in the suite. Their plan was working fine. It was a simple deal, really: The doctor gave Scranton a player who he said would help the team win, and they were winning. Undefeated. It was a long season, but Scranton was confident now. With Rotinom playing offense and defense, the team could do no wrong.

Gantriel walked off the field like he had lost. He was happy with the win, of course, but the coaches' task now just changed. They proved they could prepare well for anyone; he always had confidence in that. Now, though, he and his staff would have to serve as constant motivators and keep Cleveland ready, no matter who the opponent was. Gantriel always thought you had to be hungry to win, and it's a lot easier to be hungry when your view is looking at the top, not from the top.

Balany was clicking. He had completed 19 of 28 passes for 274 yards. He got along with his receivers, and he was the clear leader on this team. His career was peaking. The offense worked, as Carver came into his own. Balany had running and passing options like never before. And Rotinom's force on the field was never overlooked. He blocked for Balany, he menaced defenses. And he did it again and again and again.

Sails was shining in his own world, working hard to get the word out every way possible. Every statistic was studied, records that looked breakable were being mentioned. Rotinom seemed to be headed for a 300-tackle season. Balany was on track to throw 40 touchdowns. Carver was having his best year.

And the season went on in the same fashion. Few teams could threaten to score much against Cleveland because Rotinom was always there in the middle, knocking down passes and chasing runners. Offensively he created protection for Balany, opening holes "so wide a school bus could drive through, stop, pick up kids, and move on," one folksy writer penned. He moved so fast and was so strong, Balany had all the time he wanted and was rarely sacked. Riga Rotinom jerseys remained hot sellers, and the hype continued on radio airwaves, the few free ones that remained and the multitude of pay-satellite stations as well that had crept into existence years earlier. When the team hit 10-0, "Stormcats" and "championship" were beginning to be mentioned in the same breath. Clevelanders could sense a championship within reach. And unlike a perfect game in baseball, where players don't utter 'perfect game' out of revered superstition,

Stormcats fans weren't shy about mentioning the possibility of winning it all.

And in late November, when the winds off Lake Erie had started to give way to a chill that resembled winter more than fall, Andrews sat in the press box after another Stormcat win. Everyone had filed their updates and postings and interviews and analyses, and Andrews sat. She stared at the field, now empty, its grass torn in spots from the latest battle. The towering stadium lights shone on the field in the early evening. Wind whipped hot-dog wrappers and napkins between rows of seats. Her gaze followed a plastic bag that had swirled along the rows of seats, dancing up and around as if it were caught in a mini tornado.

She had spent all season watching Rotinom control almost every play, tirelessly. She saw him in the locker room, never sweating, giving his one-word answers. There was an emotionless quality to him, always. So it was with three seconds remaining against Frankfurt that Andrews had an epiphany. Her feelings and thoughts and emotions and reasoning seemed to converge in one quiet crash inside her as she stared at the depth chart before her, as the plastic bag blew around the stadium, as the field lay empty.

Riga Rotinom, she thought in the almost empty press box, I have finally figured you out.

And all she knew is that she couldn't tell anyone. At least, not yet.

CHAPTER 26

Andrews filed her dispatch and was gathering her things to leave when she stopped, holding her PDR. The tiny recorder held so much data she often told colleagues it was "my other brain, the one that remembers important things so I can retain song lyrics from 30 years ago in my head." Its memory was amazing, and its electronic filing system helpful in quickly recalling interviews she needed. In a pinch, she could even write a story on its small but functional keypad. She stared at it, hoping it would give her all the answers she needed. And, in a way, it did.

She had had a long day. So it was home again to Ginger, who got a quick meal of kibble and leftover chicken, and then on to her desk. She pulled out the card that she got at Mary-Jo's Grill, the one from Ed Register, the former colleague of Daugava's. She got him on the first ring.

"Hello, Ed? This is Catharine Andrews from The American, we met a few weeks ago at Mary-Jo's?"

"Hey, how are you? Did you ever write that story? I have to admit I don't read The American often—well, not much at all, actually. I'm not a big sports fan."

"No problem, Ed, a lot of people aren't. No, I was—I'm still gathering some notes and I got sidetracked on the season a bit."

"Oh," said Ed, a bit confused. Catharine learned something long ago, when she read "Catcher in the Rye"—say something no one understands and you'll get away with it most every time.

"The reason why I was calling is this—I often do medical stories as they relate to athletes. I want to have a voice analyzed in a lab by a technician who knows what they are doing. It's for a story on stress," she said.

"Then you want Voice Sounds Lab. I've had to go over there two or three times for a work project. They can explain all that stuff to you."

"Are they local?" Andrews asked.

"They're way out, off Interstate 90 on the way to Erie near the Pennsylvania border. VSL, they call themselves. Good outfit. The cops use them."

"Really? Excellent," Andrews said. "Hey—you got any contacts over there, someone I should ask for?"

"Yeah, there's a woman named…Robinson. What's her first name? A president's name," Ed mused. "Madison—Madison Robinson. I've worked with her; she's sharp."

"Ed, thanks—this is a huge help. I owe you a burger."

"Hey, anytime," Ed said. "Take care."

They hung up and Andrews took out her grateful feeling on Ginger, who got tossed a couple of chewy treats.

She started looking up VSL's number and then realized it was Sunday. But she called anyway and got pay dirt; the company had a phone system that allowed her to punch in the name of the person she was calling. She hit R-O-B-I, and before she got to "N" a message came on: "Madison Robinson, please leave a message."

She briefly explained who she was and that she needed someone to look over a recording she had for a story, and left her number.

The rest of the night it was Ginger, a movie, popcorn and a couple of beers from a local brewery. Cleveland had long made brewing a resurgent industry, and she liked trying the different offerings. Sunday nights caught up to Andrews. For most fans, going to a football game on Sundays meant leaving early enough to get a parking spot and walking a block or two to the game. For a player or a reporter, it meant getting there in plenty of time, and staying late. So a three-hour game turned into a full day, with interviews and writing. Watching the game was fun, but more intense. There were no cheers in the press box, only note-taking and some talking. While fans cheered or booed a big play, the media had to make notes on the particulars of the play. If a quarterback on the opposing team got sacked for a loss on a key third-down play, Andrews would note the time, who made the tackle, which offensive linemen missed a block, maybe, and other details. It was fun, but took constant attention. Before you knew it, the next play was starting. Fans standing in the cold might think an eternity had passed during timeouts, but many reporters used the time wisely.

Andrews woke on the couch, stiff-necked and surprised she slept through without waking. She took care of Ginger, always at her side, showered, and was about to make coffee when her phone rang.

"Hi, this is Madison Robinson from Voice Sounds Lab returning a call?"

"Oh, yes, thank you for calling," Andrews said, and proceeded to explain what she needed in detail. She said she didn't know how long these things took, but it was important for a story and she promised to give credit to VSL.

"I'm free at 10:30—c'mon down and let's check out this voice of yours," Robinson said in a slight Southern lilt.

"Actually," said Andrews, "I was wondering if we could make it Wednesday. Anytime. I could buy you lunch."

"I don't do lunch. But 10:30 then works, too."

It helped that Robinson's bosses were seeking publicity to get the word out on their analyses, so there would be no charge for the demonstration. Otherwise, it would have cost a bundle—a bundle Andrews was sure her editor would not have wanted to pay for her to satisfy a hunch.

The next day, Tuesday, Andrews and a host of reporters gathered after practice to talk to players. She got there early and keyed in on Rotinom, as did many reporters. He rarely spoke to reporters on practice days, but Catharine decided today she wasn't going to take no for an answer.

She made sure she was at the front of the pack, bag slung over one shoulder and her PDR thrust out.

"Riga, how is the transition to playing both ways going?"

"Fine."

"You studied the playbook a lot, right?

"Yes."

"How long?" she asked.

"Hours."

"How is your uncle doing?"

"Fine."

"What's your favorite food Riga?"

With that her press-corp brethren started groaning at the non-football question, and Catharine knew she would be razzed for it later but she didn't care.

Rotinom was silent.

"Your favorite food, what is it?"

"I don't know," he said.

With that other reporters chuckled. "Well, he ate something to make him seven-four," one said.

"Riga," Catharine continued, "what type of music do you like?"

Silence again, briefly. Then: "I don't like music."

On and on until finally another reporter jumped in with a football question. He got a one-word answer. Catharine turned and hurried out of the scrum.

The next day, she left early for the drive along the lake and found VSL. A pleasant secretary ushered her in to a lab, where a tall, thin woman in dressy slacks and a light sweater was waiting.

"Hi, I'm Catharine Andrews," she said, offering a hand.

She got a firm shake in return. "Hi, Madison Robinson."

"I expected someone in a lab coat," Andrews said.

"It's at the cleaners. But I could get my backup out, if you want."

"Not necessary," Andrews said.

"And I expected a pencil behind your ear and a reporter's notebook," Madison said.

"I can get them, if you want."

Catharine liked her. A sense of humor was always a good start.

"So, you explained a bit about what you are looking for. Do you have the recording?" Robinson asked.

"Right here," Andrews said, as she handed over the PDR, set for segments of interviews she had with Rotinom, including the one yesterday when she had gotten more out of him than ever, even if wasn't much. But she got what she needed. As Robinson set up the recording Andrews looked around. It was a giant room, with recording information and knobs everywhere, and it looked like something out of a high-tech audio-visual room at a high school.

"So you're doing a story on stress, huh?" Robinson asked.

"Yes," Andrews answered. "Trying to evaluate how stressed a football player is after a game."

Andrews wandered a bit throughout the room as Madison Robinson set up. It reminded her of a more modern version of the research area in "The Conversation," where Gene Hackman's character made specialized recordings for his job as a private detective. This office, though, was much cleaner and had a lot more light than the cavernous studio where he worked. That was one of many movies she and Ginger had seen. While many audio and video studios were digitally focused, this one had old and new technology stacked everywhere. About the only thing Catharine recognized were speakers.

"OK, we're set up," Robinson called out. "Grab a seat."

Andrews sat next to a large console of knobs and computer screens. "What we're gonna do is transfer this player's voice to computer, in what looks like a heart monitor, sort of. There's actually more complicated readings, but we'll start with this. We'll do several recordings—one you gave me of him from yesterday, and one after a game. There should be some changes between them, as he anticipates the game, and then later, when he's relieved or elated it's over."

"OK," Andrews said, keeping up.

Robinson turned a knob, typed in a few commands, then hit a key. All of a sudden Rotinom's voice sounded through several speakers.

"Yes....We must play hard....They are a very good team....No."

"Guy doesn't talk much, does he?" Robinson asked Andrews.

"No, if he gives four words it's a lot," she said.

"Are they all like this?"

"No. Some you can't get to shut up. Others talk and rarely say anything. Others you want to talk and they don't. This guy is a great player, but not one for words. English is his second language."

"Really?" asked Robinson. "I'm surprised."

"Why? Because he has no accent?"

"No, because—well, it's like this. The computer can pick up pronunciations. How the voice changes on each syllable can give us an idea of whether the person has learned English or even where he learned it."

"Really?" was all Andrews could say.

"Yeah, that's helpful in figuring out where a person is from, like a kidnapper. We help law enforcement sometimes, though most of the time we do more clinical evaluations."

"Interesting," Andrews said.

Robinson was quiet for a while, then said, "OK, this is weird."

"Weird?" Now it was Andrews who was reduced to one-word answers.

"Well…hold on, let me run this again…" Robinson seemed lost in her own world for a minute. She backed up the voice on the computer, listened again, then again.

"Say, do you mind if I call you on this? I have a glitch that has to be worked out. Might take some time."

"Umm, no problem," Andrews said, feeling like a patient whose doctor had told her the hospital needs to run more tests on her.

She thanked Robinson and walked out, feeling like she had left something uncovered. What, she didn't know.

CHAPTER 27

Tiger Canton sat under the metal bar, gripping the cold steel carefully. Fresh, white tape compressed each wrist. A random thought, recalling how he had once read his college spent $7,500 on tape alone throughout a season, ran through his head before he took a breath and lifted the bar off its holder. He exhaled as he pushed up the weight, then inhaled as he brought it down to his chest, then did it again and again as an assistant trainer spotted him. He finished his repetitions, then sat for a minute to catch his breath. Weight-room time was mandatory for all players, except Rotinom. It was one of the private deals Scranton worked out with Daugava. Gantriel didn't like it, but Scranton assured him he would work out at home while he took private English lessons, though his English seemed fine.

"You need me on more benches?" his spotter asked.

"No, I'm all right—curls now," Canton said, as he got up and walked to the rack of smaller, individual bars with weights attached. He picked one up, keeping his arm straight as he repeatedly brought his fisted grip near his chin, then back down in a smooth motion. Canton was the go-between on the team between the introverted Rotinom and everyone else. The last game, a 28-7 win over Chicago, had been closer than the score indicated, and Canton had played his heart out, as usual. It was the first time all year he had more tackles in a game than his linebacker mate. Each team tried something different against Cleveland's defense, and Chicago's approach was to stay away from Rotinom. So they tried running virtually everything Canton's way.

They forgot how good he was.

Canton moved laterally all day, pounding any runner with the ball who was able to make it through the line. At the end of the game, every piece of tape on his body was torn. Blood smeared his right forearm. A running back's hand got through his face mask early in the day, and blood trickled slowly the rest of the game. Grass stained both knees. His arms hung at his side, exhausted, when it was all over.

Now, as Canton rested between reps in the weight room days later, he didn't think of the game. He thought of being in the locker room afterward, undressing, knowing how sore he would be Monday afternoon. He didn't mind. It was still a game he was paid to play, the one he loved as a kid. But what Canton couldn't understand was Rotinom, a guy who played twice as much as he did yet never seemed to tire. Once he asked him about his workout, and Rotinom gave him that now famous thoughtful look and replied: "Cardio." Canton looked away for half a second, and when looked up to press him for details, Rotinom was gone. Another time in the locker, Canton remembered thinking, he had taken off his pads while glancing up and seeing Rotinom do the same. He had some dirt and grass on his uniform, but looked like he was ready to play more, if he had to.

Canton went back to his reps, slowly lifting the bar to his chin, slowly releasing it. He stayed lost in his thoughts, losing his count and thinking of the locker room after Sunday's game.

Later that day, Reilly Carver ran. It was his quiet time, getting a workout while he pushed himself through the hills of a neighboring county, its winding roads dipping up and down for miles at a time. He preferred to run in the parks, along trails that cut through forests and fields of grass and wildflowers, but there were too many roots and branches, too many ways to turn an ankle and end the season. So he opted for a country drive where he could run to a small village's border a few miles from where he parked his car, and back again.

Many players hated running, but Carver loved it. Maybe because no one was around, and it was only him. Maybe because it reminded him of the small town where he grew up in Iowa, though his view here was more trees than soybean or corn fields.

A light wind whipped his long-sleeved T-shirt that had one word printed upside-down on the bottom of its front. Every time Carver wiped his brow, the word came into view. He had it made specially, a reminder about the team's single goal, his goal. He ran in the left lane, facing any traffic on the recycled road, a mix of concrete, asphalt and other materials. It was fairly new and was supposed to last much longer than the old blacktop surfaces, but when you fell it felt as hard and sharp as the old roads. A comfortable sweat built up in the light layers he wore. He hit the final hill, his mind clear as he noticed the historic sign outside the village about 100 yards away. He kept his pace as the sun wore on him, until he approached it. He reached up and hit it the way players touch a lucky plaque or old football right before a game. He then turned for the second half of his run, mostly uphill back to where he left his car. His thighs burned even though he was in shape. It was a hill that, no matter how often he ran it, would always get his heart rate up. It was his workout. Every step he took, he thought, would lead to one more he could take late in a game. When the defense would tire, he would be ready. Carver would not allow himself to run out of gas—not in a game before thousands of fans, not alone on a country road.

He trudged up, sweat now pouring as he relentlessly pushed on. The Stormcats were undefeated, and Carver, as much as Gantriel or anyone, did not want to see that zero in the loss column change. Carver had an outgoing personality and got along with teammates and reporters and coaches, but deep inside a competitive fire burned. Every player had it. It was just a question of how it showed itself.

He reached the top, turning off the road into the dirt clearing where he left his car. He pulled up the shirt to wipe his brow, reading the word one more time.

"WIN."

CHAPTER 28

Andrews had finished filing an added dispatch on the latest injury report. No one was too banged up, and she wondered whether Gantriel would pull out starters even sooner than he had been doing when the game seemed in hand. Gantriel always looked so solemn on the sidelines and never really looked like a game was won, no matter what the score, until the gun sounded.

Her stomach gurgled with hunger as Ginger sat politely at her feet.

"Ohh, we're both hungry, G," she said. "Let's get you fixed up." She poured kibble, mixed it with some gravy, and set it in front of her dog. "Dinner is served, mademoiselle."

Ginger stuck her head in the bowl and inhaled the contents.

"Yeah, Ginger, chewing is overrated," she said, shaking her head.

When the phone chirped, Ginger didn't look up.

"Hello?"

"Can I speak with Catharine Andrews please?"

"Speaking."

"Hey, this is Tiger Canton of the Stormcats."

"Hey, what's up—rested after the tacklefest Sunday?"

"Yeah," Canton said, and Andrews could almost see the

smile on the other line. He had played a fantastic game, all over the field, a one-man wrecking crew. "Hey, I need to talk to you about something. It's kind of—well, I don't want to get into it on the phone, and I don't want to do it in the locker room."

"Give me a hint, Tiger." Andrews didn't date players, and there was no point in meeting Canton if he was calling to ask her out.

"It's not personal," he said, reading her mind. "It's about, it's about another player."

OK, Andrews thought, this ought to be good. She had no idea what Canton could want to talk to her about. But she had to hear what he had to say.

"You like burgers, Canton?"

"What?" he asked.

"You like burgers? You know, slab of beef between two patties, ketchup, mustard, onions, the works?"

"Well, yeah," Canton said.

"I know a place, Mary-Jo's Grill. It's off Clinton Street on the East Side."

"I'm not in an autograph-signing mood," he said.

"No fans, quiet place."

"OK," Canton said. "I'll meet you in half an hour."

"You won't regret it," she said. "Really is the best burger in the city."

"OK, I'll find it. See you there."

Andrews looked at Ginger, who looked at her with that 'Aren't we going to watch a movie and eat popcorn?' look.

"Sorry, G, I gotta go. Be good. No wild parties."

Calls from players were rare. Andrews couldn't begin to figure out what Canton wanted, but she figured any excuse to get out for another of Mary-Jo's burgers was good enough.

She had worked out on her stationary bike in the morning, rationalizing the calories she was about to enjoy.

When she got to Mary-Jo's it was fairly quiet. Faces turned and looked at her as she walked in, then they went back to their drinks, burgers, pool and jukebox. It was a Pavlovian response. When someone pushed open the door, almost everyone in the place had to look for just a second, as if they were each expecting someone. No one ever was.

Andrews walked to the bar where she saw Mary-Jo wiping glasses with a worn towel.

"The burgers are addictive," Andrews said, greeting her.

"Yeah, that they are," Mary-Jo said. "Looking for more information?"

"No, not really. Well, meeting someone. And I bragged about the burgers."

Mary-Jo smiled. Just then the door opened, and once again faces turned, then looked away. Must not be too many sports fans here, Andrews thought, since no one recognizes Tiger Canton.

Canton walked and stood next to Andrews. "Thanks for coming."

"No problem," Andrews said.

Canton looked around, almost nervous. Andrews figured out what he was thinking. "Hey, Mary-Jo, you got a quiet booth around here?"

"Sure, Catharine," she said, grabbing menus and leading them toward the back to a booth between a wall and the jukebox. It wasn't exactly private, but it would do.

"What can I get you to drink?" Mary-Jo asked as they sat. Canton waited a second for Catharine to order. Chivalry wasn't entirely dead, she thought.

"Draft," Andrews said.

"Me too," Canton said.

"You know what you want to eat?" Mary-Jo asked.

"You kidding? I've been drooling all the way over here," Andrews smiled. "Well done, and what the heck—add another slab of cheese."

"I'll have the same," Canton said.

"You got it," Mary-Jo said, turning back to the kitchen.

"You know, I stumbled across this place a while ago. Comforting, isn't it? It has that one quality I love in a restaurant."

"What's that?" Canton said.

"Someone else cooking for me," Catharine said.

Canton smiled briefly, but didn't say a word.

"OK, guy, spill it. I'm all ears," she said, then immediately felt bad about her flippant approach. All of a sudden she realized how serious Canton was, how quiet he was, and how different he seemed off the field.

"Well, it's like this. This stays between us, right? You can't tell anyone, right? I mean you can't even use this in your writing?"

"OK, we're off the record, Canton—for now. But at some point in this conversation we're going to go back on the record. Understood?"

"No," he said, "This is off the record."

Andrews sighed. Usually that declaration was accepted. Not this time. But she agreed.

"Fine. I'm all ears, and we're off the record—for now."

Mary-Jo reappeared, set down their beers and, upon seeing a quiet man stare at the table and a serious Catharine, said the burgers would be up soon and made her way back to the kitchen. She knew when to stay and joke and talk, and she knew when to clam up. It was a virtue she learned as a bar owner.

"Well, Rotinom, he, he's..." Canton looked down at his beer and let his voice trail.

Andrews decided to help him out, when appropriate. "He's a pretty good player," she said.

He looked up. "Yeah, yeah he is." He took a sip of the pilsner. Andrews could see how uneasy he was. Whatever he wanted to say, he was unsettled and she was in the dark about what it was.

"Well, you see, I pretty much know him better than anyone on the team. And that's not saying much. We don't hang out, he never goes out. And he talks in, I don't know, he rarely talks at all. You know how some guys never shut up? This guy has said maybe 50 words all year. And I probably heard 'em all."

"I've noticed," was all Andrews said.

"I mean, what I have to say, it's really crazy. You have to promise, you can't say you heard this from me."

Andrews looked up: "I promise."

Mary-Jo arrived with their burgers, and they both ate, though not with the gusto they would have if they were celebrating. Andrews wanted to change the subject for just a second, but this was the dicey part. If Canton said something usable here, quotable, it would still be off the record and she would be bound not to use it. The good thing about being off the record was it pointed a reporter toward a direction often worth looking into. The bad thing was happening now: If Canton said something Andrews wanted to use, she would have to interrupt him and get it on the record, then they would have to shift back off the record, and inevitably someone would end up "off" when the other was "on." And that was never good.

"You guys are having a heck of a season, and you're staying healthy. Makes my job a little easier."

"What do you mean?" Canton asked.

"I cover medical aspects, primarily. When a player goes down it's my job to find out about the injury, talk to doctors, other players who have had it, that kind of thing. But there's been no major injuries—knock on wood—so I have been covering the games and doing features."

"Oh," was all Canton said, putting down a half-eaten burger. He wasn't aware of who wrote what about the team. All he knew of reporters was their faces blurred out when TV folks shined those bright lights on him at his locker.

"You like the burger?" she asked.

"Yeah, it's fine. It's just, well…" Again Canton trailed off. He took a drink. Andrews could have sworn she saw his hand shake a little.

"Tiger," she said, "why don't you just tell me what it is you want. We're off the record, and if it's something I can make calls on to find out more, I will. If it's something I know the answer to, I'll answer honestly. But something's bugging you, and you've got to spit it out."

She finished by taking a sip, partly because she was thirsty and partly because she wanted to let Canton know she was done talking, for now.

Canton looked up at Andrews.

"OK," he said, taking a breath. "Here's what I think."

So he told her.

Andrews' glass slipped from her hands and shattered when it hit the old, warped tiled floor.

CHAPTER 29

Andrews barely remembered getting home that night. She felt like she was bursting to tell a secret but knew she couldn't. So she kept quiet, trying to figure an angle, something, anything to solve this problem. And it was a problem. But the next few weeks were a blur, between obsessing about what Canton had told her and traveling to Cincinnati and Pittsburgh—two more wins, keeping Cleveland's record undefeated. With the wins came more hype, as if it were needed. Cleveland now was closing in on something that had not happened in decades: An undefeated season. It was one of the most difficult challenges in all of sports. It was so easy to stumble. A key injury. A lack of focus. A fluke play. A player getting in trouble, then suspended. Something always happened, and a team always lost at least once.

But this year, Cleveland had its health and Balany leading the charges. Most of all, Cleveland had the rookie of the year and, arguably, the most valuable player, in Riga Rotinom.

The Monday before the Pittsburgh game, as Gantriel spent time in his office alone, he came to a quick decision as he rubbed his temples and nursed a cup of coffee. There would be no pep talks, no speeches. His team was undefeated. They knew it, and it was hard work and solid execution that got them there. That and he knew they were playing with heart. They wanted to win on every play. Carver had found his groove running, and Balany was doing his usual job as field leader. Every member of the defense followed Canton. Rotinom—well, he didn't say much, but he kept playing both sides of the ball.

No, Gantriel figured he would abide by the adage, "if it ain't broken, don't fix it." He would say nothing. This team knew how to win. He would spend all his time on finding ways to exploit the opponents. He would create, his team would execute.

The game against Pittsburgh almost was uneventful. Gantriel was trying desperately to pull his starters for the upcoming playoffs, but Pittsburgh had kept the game close enough to where Gantriel had to keep his first string in. It was with a minute remaining when Balany called a pitchout to Carver off tackle. One more first down and the Stormcats would have the game. Carver took the ball, swung left, and had stepped out of bounds a foot or so after the first-down marker to avoid a hit. That didn't stop a Pittsburgh lineman—frustrated all day trying to get through to Balany because he kept running into a wall with "99" on it—from slamming into Carver while both were way out of bounds. The running back flew to his left, knocking into teammates, who in the chain reaction backed into a table full of water cups. The explosion of players, table and water could be seen across the field. Sideline cameras caught the moment, and replays started immediately. Carver wasn't hurt but stunned. Players jumped up, with coaches getting in their way to stop them from getting to the defensive player who hit Carver. Everyone was yelling. A referee ran over. Gantriel hurried to the commotion.

Wayne Tarrant, Balany's backup, had a perfect view of the late hit. He threw the clipboard he was holding at Gintagle, the defensive player who lunged at Tarrant. Several Stormcats on the sidelines held back Gintagle. When Tarrant felt an arm on his shoulder he whirled around and in one motion shoved the man trying to prevent him going after Gintagle. The man tumbled backward, sending his cap flying, his microphone popping out of his shirt and his legs straight up in the air. And the cameras caught it all.

The man was a referee.

Tarrant stood stunned. He knew the gravity of what he had just done. The other officials forged in to the melee and, making sure their colleague was OK, pulled themselves into a small corner, hoping to sort the details. The tough part for the referees was most players had on ponchos; a cold December breeze had brought in a slight rain throughout the game. There were 53 seconds on the clock. Gintagle trotted back to his sidelines. A referee came out of the pile and addressed the crowd.

"There are two flags on the play..." he began.

Gantriel grimaced on the sidelines. Everyone knew what was coming.

"...personal foul, late hit, defense, number 92...."

Gantriel looked down. His other coaches stared at the referee.

"...and unsportsmanlike conduct on the Cleveland bench, number 9..."

Gantriel looked at his main backup quarterback, standing near teammates but without his clipboard.

...ejected from the game."

They lost Tarrant, and with 53 seconds remaining it didn't seem like a big deal to almost anyone but Camp

Gantriel. A quarterback, even a healthy one, was only one play from going down, and he needed to be able to count on Tarrant in case Balany went down. And Gantriel knew touching a referee was akin to a cardinal sin; this one would have consequences, and that would be an automatic one-game suspension.

Balany took a knee, and the Stormcat team that went into the locker room was subdued.

Andrews raced down from the press box with her colleagues, most of whom wanted to talk to Tarrant about what had happened on the sidelines even though the whole storyline was obvious. Tarrant acted emotionally in protecting a teammate, he violated a serious rule, and he would not be available for the team's final regular-season game. But Andrews wanted to see Rotinom before he could leave, and he always left as soon as he could. As soon as she walked in she was greeted by an explosion of pink—pink walls, pink lockers, even pink urinals. A former Pittsburgh coach had thought pink was a calming color, so he put his bachelor's degree in psychology to work by having the visiting locker room painted pink. All of it. No one knew if it worked, but it accomplished one thing: It got the other team to think of something other than the game. One coach used to cover it up with butcher paper, it enraged him so much.

Andrews wound her way through the mass of reporters and cameras to Rotinom's locker, where he was sitting calmly, already in street clothes. "The man takes the quickest shower ever," Andrews thought.

"Riga, what did you think of the penalty on the sidelines play?" she asked.

He looked up.

"Players are not permitted to touch the referee," he said. Reporters groaned. Quotes from Rotinom read like statements from a rulebook.

Canton spotted Andrews, then looked up at his teammate. He frowned when Rotinom answered.

Andrews watched as fellow reporters tried to follow up with Rotinom's opinion on the play, despite the fact he wasn't one of the players in the sideline melee. Andrews turned to Canton.

"Tiger," she said, "what did you think of the play—you were on the sidelines at the time."

"I think," he said, "it was an expected call, but I think Tarrant was sticking up for his teammate. I think that's important to note, that he didn't go off on the guy because he has a temper or anything. He was just sticking up for his guy."

Carver could not be seen by his locker. Cameras surrounded him, but his only perspective was from a guy who was hit and sent flying.

Andrews turned back at Rotinom and studied him. Never emotional. He sat still, answering questions in his usual monotone.

She looked at Canton, who was staring at her.

She filed her dispatch and drove home, actually enjoying the peace and quiet in her car. Usually she would listen to music or an automated news station reading stories from online newspapers, but today she craved solitude. She looked forward to getting home to a warm greeting from Ginger, and then she could think more about what Canton had told her at Mary-Jo's. She hit Interstate 76, which led her to the toll road, which took her into the ring of Cleveland suburbs and surrounding towns.

A few hours later she was feeding Ginger when she realized she had a phone message that had popped up earlier.

"Hi, Catharine, this is Madison Robinson from Voice Sounds Lab. I have the results of the tests we were running on the voice you gave me. Please call me as soon as you can."

PART IV

BLACK MONDAY

CHAPTER 30

Later, the tabloids and the more sensationalistic sites would call it "Black Monday."

The week leading to the Stormcats' final regular-season game, their shot at staying undefeated, started with the commissioner's office notifying Scranton first that Wayne Tarrant would be suspended for two games, which included a playoff game. Scranton had felt it would be worse and told the league office privately he would urge Tarrant not to appeal. An official was, of course, sacrosanct, and rules were rules. Sails hurried the release, which was posted on media outlets immediately along with, of course, more video of the play. Radio talk shows buzzed about it all morning, but in the end no one was really worried. After all, Tarrant had seen only "garbage time" all year; he had played only when the game was in hand, not when it was on the line.

Andrews didn't have to help her colleague Trent with the Tarrant story, so she called Madison Robinson first thing in the morning.

"I would have called sooner, but I got home late from Pittsburgh," she said.

"I have something, very odd, very strange," Robinson said, dismissing any small talk.

"I'm all ears," Andrews said.

"The voice you gave me—you're not testing me, right? It's not some sort of a joke? I mean, you're not from Quality Services, they didn't put you up to check on our work, did they?"

Andrews' confusion grew. "No, I—what do you mean?"

"I ran this voice several times through our analyses here. Through several processes that critically examine—well, basically, through the wringer. And I kept getting the same conclusion."

"Yes?" Andrews said, as she hastily poured coffee grounds into a filter.

"Well, it's like this," Robinson said, taking a breath Andrews could hear. "The voice you gave me, it's a human voice but it's a recording."

Andrews chuckled. "Of course it's a recording; I gave you my PDR, I interviewed him several times."

"No," Robinson said, "not a recording made then, a recording made before."

"OK, now I don't understand," was all Andrews could say.

This time, Andrews could sense Robinson's sigh more than her sense of urgency. "No—someone recorded a voice, and you recorded that. My data, my analyses—all of it points to a recording, not a voice coming out of someone's body. Our equipment is very sensitive, we can pick up on that."

Andrews remained quiet as she poured water and flipped the coffee maker to "on." She stood at her counter and traced the rim of her waiting coffee mug.

"It's like this," Robinson continued. "The body, in a way, muffles the voice. It's a natural occurrence in everyone, with the bones forming—well, almost a filter, sort of, for the voice. That's why everyone's voice sounds different when they hear themselves on a recording. Anyway, it comes down to this: The voice you gave me was recorded, like what you would have in an automated machine, dispensing soda or the self-serve line at the grocery. It's human, but it's been recorded. Understand?"

"Yes," Andrews said.

"What I don't understand is how it happened. You said you interviewed the player and recorded it, right?"

"That's right," Andrews said.

"I don't know," Robinson said. "I know what I heard and I know what the data says."

"What does that mean?" Andrews asked.

"It means," Robinson said as she took a breath, "either you're lying to me, or you were talking to a robot."

In that one sentence, Andrews' uncertainty vanished. A smile replaced her frown.

"Madison," she said, "can you make sure you send me a copy of your data right away? Your conclusions?"

John Balany had driven to his financial adviser's office in the morning before having to watch film of the Pittsburgh game. He had a quick meeting in his adviser's swanky fourth-floor office that sat on the Cleveland border with the East Side suburbs. Balany needed to pick up some documents about a company he was thinking of investing in, but he also wanted to sign several footballs for a charity auction his adviser was coordinating.

Balany carried a box of footballs in his left arm as he stepped into the elevator, his mind on all the game film he would have to watch—first of the Pittsburgh game, then he would get a head-start on Atlanta, the team's final opponent. The fact about the Atlanta game that Balany and the coaches and the reporters and most fans knew was this:

Even though Cleveland already was locked into making the playoffs because of their record, winning meant being undefeated. But the bigger challenge was Atlanta. A loss would send them home, no playoffs. A win, though, would keep them alive. Cleveland wanted to win. But Atlanta needed to win.

Balany hit the down button and stood alone, facing the elevator door as it started to close.

"Excuse me!" Balany was startled out of his thoughts by a woman running to the elevator. "Can you hold the door?"

His instincts took over. Instead of punching the "door open" button, he quickly stuck out his free hand to reverse the door closing, but it didn't stop.

"C'mon," Balany muttered to himself, waiting for the door to open, since his hand had stopped the motion.

But it didn't. It shut on his hand, and now squeezed tighter. Balany felt the elevator jolt slightly; it was starting to move.

"What the —" Balany said, dropping the box of balls so he could grab his right wrist to try to pull his hand out. But the elevator door closed tighter. Where there should have been a black-rubber cushion there was just metal. He could feel his knuckle being squeezed and something grazing and pushing on his fingers. He couldn't reach the "door open" or emergency button on his right. He kept pulling at his wrist, but he felt something crack.

"Noooo!" he screamed, pulling even harder until he finally came free and flew backward, hitting the back wall with a thud. He cradled his right hand and saw his knuckle was red and swelling fast. He couldn't move his middle finger, and lines of blood formed in scratches all over his hand and wrist.

Scranton was just leaving his office when the call came from the hospital: Balany's hand was crushed. He had broken two metacarpals. It was being iced, but doctors quickly figured he would need an operation to insert pins to hold a bone in place, then a cast. He heard a doctor tell him "metacarpal" and "phalange" but the words rolled over him. The doctor must have been a Stormcat fan, because Scranton never had to ask which hand.

"It's his throwing hand, Mr. Scranton," the doctor said.

Scranton stood, alone at his desk. Usually he would have taken furious notes and then let Sails flush them out for a press release after he gathered his staff for a "reaction" meeting, as he called them. Not this time. His star quarterback was done. He would contact the team docs to have them head to the hospital to confer, but that was meaningless. A quarterback who has to take dozens of snaps to grip a football repeatedly over the course of a game would not be able to with Balany's injury.

Scranton knew Balany was finished for the season. But the worst part was it took him a minute to realize the first piece of news made it worse: Tarrant's suspension. So he couldn't rely on his No. 2 quarterback, either.

By the time Scranton received the news about Balany and had Sails draft the release, the players had finished watching films and had gone their separate ways. Gantriel had been given a message from the front office that Balany "had an accident" and would not be attending films. Gantriel immediately dispatched an assistant to see how bad. The assistant came back as players had left and gave Gantriel the news.

"Get Joey Bexar in here early tomorrow," Gantriel said, referring to the third-string quarterback who had not taken a snap all year. "I mean crack of dawn. We have a lot of work to do."

Bexar—pronounced BAY-yer—was a kid out of Texas, a second-year player with a strong arm and great speed, who showed flashes of promise. The coaches had thought about converting him to defensive back but they did that with their fourth-string quarterback Cuya Aconttie who, technically, was listed as fourth-string but who spent time at various positions, even helping out on the scout team. Aconttie had played quarterback in college, but it was clear he would be converted to kick returner and safety when he made the NPL.

The rules allowed teams to carry as many quarterbacks as they wanted, but had to follow their depth charts when inserting them into games. Anyway, that didn't matter; Gantriel didn't have either of his top two quarterbacks available.

Bexar had issues. One problem was discipline. He had shown up late for two practices during the beginning of the season, and once the coaches had caught him nodding off during films.

Another problem was motivation. It was difficult to get motivated when he knew he would not play. He actually liked to handle the clipboard on the sidelines, to have something to do. Bexar was around to watch and learn to be ready, but Bexar was bored. And Bexar's problem was, at times, attitude.

A single guy, he knew no one in Cleveland, or all of Ohio for that matter, except for a second cousin, a nightclub owner who introduced him to some people. Bexar preferred different clubs than ajo and hung out with almost no one on the team. And so after watching films, Bexar quickly put on street clothes and headed to a place on the West Side of town, down near the river, where he could enjoy dinner and maybe have a drink or two while watching the night game. His cousin had promised to fix him up with a woman who he said was a big football fan, but Bexar found out in less than five minutes she didn't know a fumble return from a kickoff return. No matter; she was pretty and he was out, enjoying the night. And she had no idea he hadn't played a down all season. For all she knew, he could have told her he was the team's star and she would have believed him.

He ordered a round of chicken wings, the house specialty, and a couple of drinks, alternately talking with his date, Monique, and keeping an eye on the game. Bexar kept drinking and watching, and before he knew it the clock ran down for halftime. By the time the third quarter started the alcohol was having its effect. Monique left in a huff over something he had said, but by the time the clock ticked into the fourth quarter he couldn't remember what it was. He ordered another drink. With 10 minutes remaining in the game, he didn't care. He got another drink.

When the game wound down Bexar felt sleepy and his head was starting to pound. He needed rest. He dropped a handful of bills to cover his tab, then headed out. He swayed a bit as he walked, steadying himself on chairs as he staggered to the back entrance. He didn't feel like being recognized by anyone, he was tired and wanted to get home. For some reason, he reached into a small bowl left on someone's table next to a plate of bread and scooped out a handful of individually wrapped butter slices. He shoved them in his pocket.

No one saw Bexar leave since he walked out the back door. It was after midnight. The cold air hit his face in a quick eye-opening moment as he fumbled for his keys. He swayed to his car, the moonlight shimmering across the river as he got in.

"That's the lake," he slurred to no one. "The lake is always north."

As he wheeled out of the lot he looked up and could see the city lights. He pulled the wheel left and found himself on a steep, curving road. Immediately it wasn't familiar. Uh-oh, he thought, wrong way.

He drove up the road a ways, then pulled over as far as he could to the right to swing around. But what Bexar didn't see was a car coming down the road right at him. What happened next came so fast the other driver and Bexar could not react, not even swerve. Bexar was making the U-turn on a curve, and then BOOM! He slammed the other driver, sending the car down a short hill. It rumbled and bounced downward, landing with a thud, then a groaning, hissing sound.

Bexar's car was off the road in a small ditch, and he just sat there, groggy, though unhurt.

Almost immediately lights were flashing and police and an ambulance were all around him, and an officer was talking to him, but he could not understand.

"Sir, sir, can you hear me!?"

Bexar looked up, the blinking bright lights flashing all around him it seemed, reds and blues on the otherwise darkened road.

"Wha, what happened, I was jes drivin' and —"

The cop looked up and said something into his walkie-talkie, then looked back to Bexar, asking him if he were hurt and how much he had to drink. Another officer came over, and the two helped Bexar out of the car. Bexar tripped, and nearly fell, but the officers caught him. There would be no sobriety test; Bexar could barely stand, and could barely make out what anyone was saying. Commotion surrounded him, with people talking and uniformed people moving up and down the hill. And the flashing lights, they seemed to be constant, but Bexar didn't know where they were coming from. He heard shouts and directions but could not make them out as he felt his arms being tugged behind him and cold metal clicking on his wrist. It seemed like no one—including the two officers next to him—were paying any attention to him; they were all down the hill or looking in that direction.

"How bad!?" he heard someone yell as he blinked, the lights not stopping.

Suddenly the officer's walkie-talkie crackled and he turned, speaking into it softly. When he turned back, Bexar felt his arms being pulled sharply, and he almost tripped. Both officers gripped his arms tight as they pulled him away and shoved him roughly into the back of a police cruiser nearby.

Hey, wha the—"

"SHUT UP!" an officer yelled as he slammed the door.

The lights kept flashing, illuminating him as if he were on a club's dance floor—red, blue, red, blue, red, blue. They wouldn't stop.

Joey Bexar didn't know it then, but the car he hit had been a police cruiser.

CHAPTER 31

S cranton's long day was getting longer.

It was almost 1:30 a.m., and his wife was asleep. His mind couldn't stop racing: Tarrant's suspension, Balany's injury. He had been on the phone with the coaches and doctors all day. Not only did a chance at remaining undefeated look slim, but Scranton now worried about the subsequent playoffs without a veteran quarterback. Scranton's phone rang as he was walking upstairs. He took the call, sighed as he heard the story, then clicked off. He turned around and walked back downstairs. He would have more calls to make. A lot of calls.

Bexar was booked and would remain in jail until morning when a lawyer would accompany him before the judge at a bond hearing. After that he would be released, since he had no prior record, but the bond would be high. And while he technically could practice with the team and even play on Sunday, Scranton felt that would be distracting and disrespectful. The officer Bexar hit was in bad shape and remained in a coma. No way could Bexar take the field while a cop laid in a hospital bed.

It was all up to Cuya Aconttie.

Aconttie had not come from a big-name college or factory. He was always just barely making teams. He had been a walk-on in college, earned a starting job, then had a good enough senior season to get some looks from scouts. He had been an undrafted free agent and spent two years trying to make pro teams, only to get cut in the final paring, that time in training camp when the last few players are let go. But Gantriel and the other coaches saw something in Aconttie. He had some speed, but was never the fastest. Good hands, though never the flashiest player around. But what Gantriel liked best was his attitude. Always upbeat, always working. When the coaches approached him about converting to defense and becoming a safety, he simply said: "Sounds fun; let's do it." So he had made the team and would fill in for injured Stormcats in the secondary—the defensive backs and safeties whose primary job was to guard the opponents' receivers. He saw the game from a new perspective.

It was almost 2 a.m. when Scranton called Gantriel and broke the news about Bexar. The team would have no choice. Aconttie, who had never taken a snap in a game, would play quarterback Sunday when the Cleveland Stormcats played their biggest game of the year. No pressure: A loss would blow an undefeated season and send them into the playoffs looking as human as all other teams.

Gantriel went into his study and stared at a display-case football, autographed from a playoff team from a few years back. It was his best team to date. He sat in his chair and stared at that football for a long time before closing his eyes and wondering how, when everyone thought he had all the answers and all the plays and all the players, he would get a fourth-string quarterback ready to play in less than a week.

Catharine Andrews, tired of tossing in bed and unable to sleep, got up. Ginger shook and groggily followed her to the living room, hoping food might be involved in this late-night endeavor. Ginger sighed when Andrews plopped herself into the couch and flipped on the television. "It's a Wonderful Life" came on, in its black and white glory, one of the many showings of the holiday season. She had seen it a dozen times, but she was glad to find an old movie she could stare at and, hopefully, turn off and go back to bed soon.

The movie was near the beginning. A frantic young George Bailey faced his childhood dilemma—knowing his boss, Mr. Gower, had accidentally mixed the wrong pills for a patient. Ginger had hoisted herself up in slow-motion it seemed, she was so tired, and curled up on the couch. Andrews stroked her dog as she tried to think what to do next. She had no idea. She had a lot of information that pointed to a weird conclusion, felt she had to tell someone important, but didn't know who. She thought about Sails. That idea was out. The team would prepare a statement. Preparing a statement always seemed to be the team's answer. Scranton, maybe. The buck stopped with him. Gantriel. She had a few one-on-ones with Gantriel over the years. He remained reserved but had been fair.

She watched as the old druggist, Mr. Gower, yelled at George to deliver the medicine. George looked around the store and saw an advertisement sign that said "Ask Dad—he'll know." Heavy overshadowing, but it was all George needed.

And it was all Catharine needed. She picked up her cell phone and dialed a speed number.

"Hello?" a voice answered on the first ring.

"Hey dad, it's Katie," she said.

Almost half an hour later, Andrews felt relief. Relieved her dad lived in California, where the time difference allowed her to catch him before he went to bed. And relieved that, as always, her dad made her feel better.

In the morning, somehow, she would try for an interview with Nevada Collins, the league's commissioner. It was a two-pronged challenge. First she would have to convince her editor to authorize her to travel, an expense he might not be willing to make since she was taking a flier on an interview. And second, she would have to convince Collins to sit for an interview.

She woke early and called her editor, even before glancing at the messages popping up in her news feed. No greeting. Usual gruff beginning. She realized he probably hadn't finished coffee yet.

"So my second call of the day is from one of my reporters, who wants to go to New York to interview the commissioner in person."

"That's right, Todd. I wouldn't ask if it weren't important. You see, I—"

"Yes, it's important. Go. Today. Leave your medical-expert cap, pack your legal-expert one. Find out about the legality of whether Bexar could play Sunday, if he had to. Find out—"

"Todd, what are you talking about?" Andrews asked.

"You haven't heard?"

"I'm as far from a cup of coffee as you are, Kelly."

"Joey Bexar got drunk last night and smashed into a cop car, nearly killed the officer. The guy's in a coma, Bexar is in jail. Arraignment is in three hours. I'm having Trent go to that, since he lives close to downtown and is right by the jail. You come to New York, talk to Collins, find out everything about where the league stands on this. Talk to lawyers—how do you defend him? Who will defend him—the league or the team? Does insurance figure in? Catharine, I haven't had my second cup of coffee and I already have all these questions."

Andrews smiled as she glanced for a notebook and pen. "Got it," she said. "I'll grab my stuff and head to the airport in 20 minutes."

"OK," he said. Hustle up. Come back tonight. If you have to stay till tomorrow, that's OK, but try to hustle on this. This team has had no controversy all year, now they have to deal with this."

"Are you going to try to—"

"Yes," he said, anticipating her question. "I'll have Trent try for an interview with Bexar, though I think I have a better chance of starting at quarterback this week than he does of getting the interview. I'll have one of the other guys get to Aconttie, also."

"Sounds good," was all Andrews could say. She wasn't best buddies with her editor, but he had things under control.

"Hey," Kelly asked, "why did you call?"

"Clairvoyant, boss, anticipating your call," she said, and hung up.

CHAPTER 32

Andrews had just one wish when she traipsed from the airport through the streets of Manhattan to the commissioner's office in midtown: That it wouldn't snow. As much as she loved snow, she had no overnight clothes, no toothbrush, nothing. She took her purse, laptop and PDR. That was it. It was her quickest packing job ever. When she was a young reporter she heard stories about reporters who kept an overnight bag in the trunk for sudden out-of-town trips, but those days were long gone. A snowstorm socking in the airports would strand her.

She found Collins' office, not far from Central Park. Andrews had run through the park on other trips here, but no time today. Today she didn't even have to wait when she got to Collins' office, and she was ushered into a spacious room immediately. Everything was big about the room—the lush, leather chairs, the windows overlooking the almost-always busy Manhattan streets, the desk that looked bigger than a pool table. And it wasn't until Collins stood and extended his bear claw of a hand that Andrews realized she had forgotten he was a former offensive lineman. His physique had given way to that common pear shape that takes over so many men in their 50s, but he hadn't let too much weight sag at him. He looked comfortable in a crisp white shirt with no tie and a blue blazer in his office, which surprisingly was lined with more art prints than football mementos.

She had managed to convince the commissioner to sit down without anyone present, and that in and of itself was a feat. Usually CEOs and the like had an entourage at their heels, with at least one lawyer in the bunch.

After the niceties, they got down to business. Collins knew why she was there—well, half the reason. And neither liked small talk. Collins calmly walked her through how the league would treat Bexar's arrest, and there were no surprises. The league had partnered with law enforcement on several marketing occasions, and trying to fight this—one of its players accused of slamming into a cop while drunk—well, the only way to face it was directly. So Collins said all the right things—he offered thoughts and prayers for the injured officer and his family, the team would handle all of Bexar's legal bills, which would come out of Bexar's salary, and no way would he play Sunday. He said the league would pay for Bexar to get in an alcohol-awareness program, but off the record he said a judge eventually would order that and no way did he foresee a trial. Collins wasn't stupid; earlier he had talked with Scranton and laid down the law.

Then Catharine had to broach the subject she was there for. She had the plane ride to think of the tack she would take. The main goal—well, one of them—was not to come off sounding like a crazed person.

"Nevada, thanks for all the frank information about the Bexar accident. Now, there's one other issue I need to bring up, and then I'll get out of your hair."

"Heck, Miss Andrews, there ain't much up top here to get out of, hehh hehh," the balding Collins drawled. When

Collins wasn't under fire his drawl seemed to come out a bit more pronounced. "Fire away."

"Well, it's like this: I am going to bring up a crazy scenario about the Stormcats, a team I have covered for several seasons, and I want to ask what the league office thinks of it."

He chuckled. "It's a buildup, Miss Andrews, I'm listening."

"Bear with me just a minute, sir, until I can get to the punchline. I can't hit you over the head with the proverbial frying pan until I get all the eggs in it."

Andrews could talk folksy with the best of them.

Collins smiled, but said nothing.

Catharine took a deep breath and began: "As you know Riga Rotinom has had an amazing season."

Collins brightened. "Boy has he. That player never gets tired. Wish I had his energy."

Catharine had planned more of a windup to her questions, but all of a sudden she started to feel like she was about to get a shot in a doctor's office, and had the urge to get it over with.

"Well, that's the problem, sir."

"What do you mean?" Collins asked.

Catharine had thought this part through. She knew her football history.

"Sir, do you remember your final game?"

"Of course I do, Miss Andrews."

"Sir, I have seen that game and I have watched it and stared at the postgame interviews over and over."

Collins was silent. Andrews kept going.

"You gave your heart and soul in that game. I know your rep was to never take it easy on any play, but that game—that game you really pushed yourself. I read how you said it was part adrenaline and part refusal to lose. I watched how you pushed not only yourself but your teammates. You were emotionally charged. You gave a damn. Afterward, with the cameras rolling, I remember watching the blood and dirt on your forehead, saw you holding an ice pack, and heard a reporter say you went out with your greatest game ever."

Collins stared at her and said two words: "We lost."

"I know," she said, "but even as a young girl who wasn't at the game, I knew you were a player who gave his all. You left nothing on the field. Even I could see that."

Collins was silent for a moment, then said quietly: "Thank you."

"He's not real," Andrews said.

"Excuse me?" Collins asked.

Andrews breathed in to steady herself and repeated what she had said. "Riga Rotinom is not real. He doesn't get tired because he's a machine. You can't play 60 minutes of this game and not be a little tired. Not be a little emotional. Not be a little bloody."

She paused, studying Collins. She had told herself on the plane to remember to check Collins' face to see if he had any inkling about this, but her gut told her he was clueless. Either way it was going to be a tough interview. If he knew, he was covering something. If he didn't know, he was duped. Either way, she was the messenger, and he wasn't going to be happy, and messengers usually take the brunt in situations like this.

Collins smiled slowly, unnerving Catharine. The last thing she wanted here was to be patronized. She was ready for that response, though. She looked at her phone. "I have 10 minutes remaining, and I promised not to take any more of your time," she said. "But I found out a few things you might want—should—hear." She continued without waiting for a response.

"I believe Riga Rotinom is a machine, created by a retired engineer named Daugava, Janis Daugava. He was—is—an expert in robotics. Rotinom is not a man—a man sweats in a locker room after going both ways on a football field. As a matter of fact it's impossible not to sweat in the humid temperatures of a locker room. Even reporters do. But not Rotinom. I've seen him all year. Never sweats. Never been cut. Not on grass, not on turf, not a scratch. Goes both ways for almost every second of a 60-minute game, not a drop of blood on him. His voice? Not human. I had a lab analyze it. Can't come from a human body; it's 100 percent computerized. That's been checked and rechecked by an independent lab.

"I have seen this guy. He doesn't even breathe deep. Daugava had years to perfect this and access to technology, and he pulled it off," Andrews said. "And in that time, of working alone on this, this project, he also honed his back story. Riga is from Latvia, where records can't be traced. Raised in an orphanage, which no longer exists.

"Sir, I am telling you, Janis Daugava created Rotinom."

Andrews took a deep breath and waited for Collins' reaction.

"That's quite a theory, Miss Andrews," he said, the drawl gone.

"Yes, sir."

Collins turned in his chair, wanting to scream and laugh as loud as he could. But if he did, Andrews could write something—anything—about this, and while she might look like a crackpot, that would make the commissioner's office look bad. And he couldn't have that.

"OK, Miss Andrews, your cat's out of your bag. But I can't comment. I can ask about it, and sound crazy, but I will. But no official comment."

"I guess I don't have a lot of expectations of what you would do, sir, I just wanted to bring this to your attention before I write anything."

"When would that be?"

"Not sure. But I would figure that having an ineligible player on the field—and I think a cyborg would qualify as ineligible—would be a problem. Cleveland is going for the undefeated mark Sunday, and I…" Andrews let her voice trail. In truth, she wasn't sure when she would write what she had. Or even IF Kelly would let her. She started doubting her decision not to tell her editor the whole reason why she had wanted to go to New York to interview Collins. She had thought it a stroke of luck that he had sent her anyway. Now she regretted it. She had only one ace remaining, and she didn't plan to pull it out now.

"OK, Miss Andrews," Collins repeated. "I'll take it to the team. Everything starts with honesty, I suppose, so a point-blank question from me can't hurt. Is there anything else?"

Andrews hesitated. "No, nothing else," she said. "I'll await your call."

CHAPTER 33

Andrews filed from the airport, then settled in for the plane ride back to Cleveland. No snow, no delays. Despite being petite, she squirmed in the tiny seat. Coach class hadn't evolved at all over the years, seats remaining tight as two coats of paint. She thought about what she knew and what she had to do. She had to tell Kelly. She had to go to Scranton, at some point. And she had to figure out a better way to tell these people her theory, she thought, or they would look at her like she had a football for a brain.

By the time she woke Wednesday morning in Cleveland snow had started to fall. She took an excited Ginger, forgetful her owner had left her with a sitter for the day before, for a walk. She brewed coffee, took a deep breath, and called Kelly. She had to get this over with sooner than later.

He answered on the first ring.

"Kelly."

"Hey, it's Andrews."

"OK, good, good work on the Bexar piece. We're on top of that. Moral of the story: Don't drink and drive if you want to play football on Sunday," he said.

"Yeah," Andrews said. "Listen, I need to talk to you about something else."

"Go," said Kelly, all business.

Andrews breathed deep and tried to avert any interruptions. "Todd, let me get this one out, OK? I'll tell you everything."

"I'm listening," he said, a bit more somber than glib this time.

Andrews then launched into her tale, her theory, about how no way Rotinom was human. She knew Kelly wouldn't be as polite as Collins, that she would have questions to fend. She finished and waited for his response.

"Well," he said, "makes sense to me."

"Really?" Andrews asked. She had anticipated being humored, being told she needed help.

"Sure," he said. "Guy has about a kajillion sacks AND goes both ways AND—don't forget this one—he has never been penalized all year. Has to be a machine."

"You're, um, taking this kind of well," Andrews said.

"And all this time I thought you wanted to go to New York to shop, not to interview Collins."

Andrews let the stereotypical comment pass, knowing he didn't really mean it.

"We have just one problem, Catharine."

"What's that?"

"You can't write it."

"Why?" Andrews asked.

"Let me put my devil's-advocate hat on," he said. "Speculation. I need his head on a platter, so to speak. Nothing you say is more than a theory, except the voice analysis, but that alone won't do it. Think about it: You're going to write a story accusing the team—and by extension, the league—of this outlandish, crazy claim, and with what proof?"

Andrews smiled.

"I got proof," she said.

"You kind of buried the lead there, Andrews," said Kelly, using the journalistic cliché about not getting to the point of a story right away.

And then she told him her ace in the hole.

After she hung up, she had more calls to make. Scranton, then Daugava. Scranton's secretary said the owner was out of his office and wouldn't be back today. Andrews thought that odd, since he was more of the tied-to-the-desk owner rather than the get-out-and-schmooze owner so many teams seemed to have. Daugava didn't answer. She drove by the diner. Not there, either.

She decided to write what she had, to be ready when she did finally talk to Scranton and Daugava and, of course, Rotinom. That would be a fun one, she thought. "Did you always want to be a robot? Which robot from the movies is more realistic? Do you need oil like the Tin Man?"

Andrews had no idea why any of this appeared funny now. In four days, Cleveland would be playing the biggest game of its season. They had a fourth-string quarterback in. That fact was reported and re-reported every day leading to the game. That storyline would shift quickly, though, to a different one when Andrews' story broke: Would Rotinom play?

She finished writing, then took a quick break to get her eyes off of her laptop, then read it again. She found the fresh vantage helped her catch typos. "Reax," editors' shorthand for reaction, was all she needed as a name. And what a reaction it would be.

She and Ginger enjoyed spaghetti and an old movie, then it was off to bed. She dreamed of a thousand mechanical arms in a factory, all throwing footballs over and over. There was no plot, no people, no talking in her dream. Just repetition. She woke early and hadn't even had a chance for coffee when her phone buzzed.

"Hel, hello," she mumbled groggily.

"I'm coming to Cleveland tomorrow," Kelly said, in his typical to-the-point manner. "There's going to be a sitdown at Emerald Lake—you, me, Collins, Scranton, Daugava. No one else as far as I know, but I bet a couple of attorneys will be there. I need you to be ready for that meeting."

In the few seconds it took Kelly to get the words out, Andrews had woken.

"Yes," she said, "Ready."

CHAPTER 34

The rest of the day was a blur. Andrews was back at practice, following the team as best she could, checking on players' medical reports. She swung by Mary-Jo's and grabbed a burger with bacon—she didn't like bacon but she knew a certain dog who would love the treat. When Mary-Jo found that out she told Andrews she would put on an extra slice next time. The two had become friendly in her jaunts for information. Andrews even shot a game of pool against a guy from Zadrandall, and didn't mention Daugava. The whole night, as a matter of fact, she didn't mention him or Rotinom or the Stormcats. She was at ease.

But her subconscious wasn't comfortable. That night she had a restless sleep, dream after dream—nothing overt, just repetitive motions again involving footballs, but with no plot or people she recognized.

She arrived early for the meeting and sat in her car gathering her thoughts as she sipped from an old travel cup. The words "Light" and "We're Your Paper" were fading over an image of a rolled-up newspaper. She collected different newspaper mugs and cups, and had come across this one at a garage sale years earlier. She and Kelly agreed to meet in the lot, and she saw his rental pull in as she drained the last bit of coffee, as if it were a shot of courage for someone in a bar.

She got out of her car and let Kelly see her. He parked and walked over, stopping momentarily to notice the giant Stormcats logo stenciled in the lot. It was as big as a basketball game's half-court team logo.

"They don't miss a beat with their marketing messages, eh?" he said.

"Nope," Catharine replied.

They talked, going over their game plan, but it wasn't really a complicated effort. They were going to lay out what she had and get comment. That was the goal, a simple goal.

She flashed her media credential and Kelly signed in, and they were escorted to a meeting room. Everyone was waiting. Only Daugava rose, always the gentleman. They sat, with Collins at the head of a large, long oak table in the small conference room where they gathered. A well-dressed man and woman sat on the outside of the table and were introduced as lawyers for the league. Andrews and Kelly exchanged a "no surprise" look

As Andrews sat she couldn't help notice the black and white framed photographs along the wall. Every other one was an 8-by-10 shot of a former front-office person, alternating with action shots of Stormcats from years past. Andrews had heard about this room. Scranton himself was behind the layout. The reasoning, supposedly, lay in the theory that it took a solid team in the front office to get the one on the field ready. Andrews thought it was a nice idea, but it still came down to the guys in the trenches who had to pound the ball for one more first down in the fourth quarter. Or the guys who could streak down the sidelines and catch a pass in stride, like LeBon or Wisgenti. Or tight ends like Culpepper who had the guts to run across a defense and wait for the catch, knowing they could be leveled by a defensive player. And guys like Canton, who gave their all every Sunday because deep down it was their love of the game that drove them.

So it was that just a little anger rose in Andrews, who had been too busy chasing the story to have much of an opinion either way. This was cheating, pure and simple, to have a fake player out there. An illegal edge making it unfair to every man on the field. She had told Kelly the day before she was ready for the meeting, and in a way she was, she had prepared what she needed. But it wasn't until she sat down in this room that she was really ready. An editor of hers had said years earlier "Write when you're mad; edit when you're calm." She thought of that as she glanced at the wall of photos.

She pulled out a notebook and her PDR. Daugava moved a little in his seat.

"Just to be clear," Kelly said, "We're on the record today."

Daugava moved again, but Collins spoke with a gentle smile. "Fine," he said.

Good call, Todd, she thought.

Scranton spoke first.

"Miss Andrews, the commissioner has told me of your claim. To call it, well, 'outlandish' just scratches the surface, I'm sure you'd agree. Rotinom is in tremendous shape, and has been his entire life. This business of him not sweating in the locker room, I honestly don't think that proves anything."

"What about his voice?" Kelly piped up.

Scranton turned to Daugava and smiled. Andrews got an odd sense in her stomach. "I'll let the doctor discuss that."

Daugava turned to the end of the table where Kelly and Andrews were sitting.

"When he was in his late teens, Riga had a tiny growth on his vocal cords removed. The growth was benign, but doctors had to attach a partial artificial implant. I am not a medical doctor, but I do believe this may account for his voice not looking like a typical person's voice, at least according to a lab analysis."

Scranton nodded and jumped back in the discussion.

"And the business of Rotinom never getting cut. Miss Andrews, I am sure you know the extent to which the league has developed its fields. These are not cheap turf surfaces. Part of their design was to protect players as well as be able to stand up to the constant pounding. Better turf means fewer injuries," he said. "The hybrid grass that was created a few years ago to grow with limited light indoors is a blessing to players."

Collins cleared his throat.

"Miss Andrews," he said, "You kept your eyes open, you studied carefully, and I don't doubt your abilities to observe. The only problem I have is in your conclusions."

Kelly looked to Andrews, who soaked it all in. She had taken a few notes, but basically the conclusion to draw here is that she was being patronized. It was clear, she thought: Collins instructed Scranton not to level any criticism at her. They would state their case politely, then it would go away.

But it wasn't going to go away.

"Anything more?" she heard a voice. But it wasn't one of the league officials hurrying the meeting; it was Kelly.

"Yes," she replied. "There is this."

With that Andrews reached down and pulled out a small plastic bag and put it on the table. It held an odd-looking, tiny microchip, one with a right angle.

"This was found, and given to me. I am not an expert but it has, I am told, some interesting characteristics. We had it tested, and it's…" she said, leaving a pause hang a second for effect, "… very advanced."

Kelly and Andrews surveyed the room. Daugava asked to see the chip.

"Where did you get this?" Scranton asked.

"It was found on the field."

Scranton started to say something, then Daugava leaned forward and whispered to Scranton.

Kelly leaned and moved in closer to Andrews for his own private caucus. "I've got nothing to say, but I want to let them think I'm telling you something important right now," he whispered. "Nice job. And nice source work."

Andrews smiled inside. Kelly had been right, at first, that everything she guessed about Rotinom was just that—a guess. Until Canton had reached into his pocket that night at Mary-Jo's and gave her the chip.

It was just a tackle on a typical play, nothing special, he had said, one of many he and Rotinom had made one Sunday, and one that stopped the defense cold on third down late in the game. But as he pushed himself off the ground, he felt a slight, sharp prick on the part of his palm that was exposed after tape had worn off. He looked down and saw the chip stuck to his hand. Any other object—a pebble, anything—he simply would have brushed away. But the odd, L-shaped triangle, the sharp edges—something made him tuck it under his wristband, he had said.

Andrews had told him it could be from the football, part of the chips used to see if a ball had crossed the plane on goal-line stands. Canton said he wondered that too, except later, in the locker room, he had seen a small puncture wound, more of a slit, on Rotinom's forearm. Same size and shape as the chip. And with no blood. And that's when he started putting two and two together, he had told her.

Canton and Andrews, it seemed, had separately come to the same conclusion about Rotinom.

Scranton fidgeted as he turned to where Collins sat, and Andrews thought she could make out what he said privately to the commissioner: It's real.

Collins quickly narrowed his eyes at Scranton before clearing his throat. Andrews watched carefully. Collins was not happy with Scranton. The commissioner then asked if Andrews and Kelly could leave the room for a moment. Andrews didn't know what to say. She wasn't accustomed to being dismissed. She needed Kelly's lead. So when her editor said "Let's go," she picked up her things and started to move for the door. But Kelly walked to the head of the table. He picked up the baggie, then made his way to the door.

"Let us know when the caucus is over," he said.

When they got outside, Andrews breathed deep. "Good call on getting the chip," Andrews said.

"Well," Kelly said, "they don't know we have a 3D copy, but nonetheless."

"I feel like a coach waiting for a play to be reviewed," Andrews said.

Kelly smiled. "Something like that."

"I'd like to be the proverbial fly on the wall," Andrews said.

"Doesn't matter," Kelly said.

"Why?"

"If they let us stay in there, and Collins spoke, that would mean he knew about this. But the fact we got temporarily dismissed means Scranton kept this from him. This was all Scranton and Daugava. Collins is telling Scranton what to say and probably praying they can control Daugava."

She hadn't thought that far ahead, but she figured her editor probably was right. The door opened, and one of the lawyers popped his head out for Andrews and Kelly. After they sat again, almost everyone had eyes on Collins.

"Get your pen out, Miss Andrews."

And the story was told.

CHAPTER 35

Collins looked bad. He hadn't known about the scam. Scranton looked to be in trouble. He had cheated everyone—from the fans to his fellow owners, neither of whom would be all that forgiving. Daugava was out the rest of the money from the contract he signed with Scranton. But he figured within a day of the story, the U.S. military would be calling. Rotinom was the most advanced robot, cyborg—whatever you wanted to call him, or it, anyone had seen. What's more, he was battle-tested. And Daugava hadn't broken any laws, either. Just rules.

Andrews recorded and took notes, and for once was glad an editor was present, because Kelly tossed in a few questions along the way. She had her story, which was being spilled out now all around her. It was clear Collins had told Scranton to sit for this interview and take the blame, and he did. One of the first questions Catharine had was whether Gantriel had any knowledge of the scheme. Scranton shook his head no. That gratified Andrews, who didn't see the coach as a cheater.

The other question was what would happen to Scranton. A massive fine and suspension, Collins said, though the amounts would have to be considered and announced in coming days. Daugava would disappear.

So the volley of questions and answers brought a rush of information that didn't stop for an hour. No, the league knew nothing of Daugava's plan; yes, Daugava did this on his own; no, the league did not condone cheating; yes, Scranton said, he thought it would change the league and eliminate injuries down the road, if teams could use such robots. And yes, at the beginning of the season he felt Rotinom would have the impact he did. No, none of the players knew anything. The only one who knew was Scranton. The story on Rotinom's background was entirely fiction, of course, concocted and fine-tuned by Daugava while he toiled away on his project. The doctor was from Latvia, but that's as far as the truth went.

And so it went, Andrews flipping her notebook to a fresh page every minute or so as she glanced at her recorder to make sure it was still running. Her story would be picked up by everyone, complete with video of the chip that The American would provide.

Later, Collins would call Gantriel, and the old coach would fall back in his chair, stunned. But deep down he would realize he shouldn't have been. Though Gantriel rarely showed emotion, he had been amazed by Rotinom all year. Went both ways, never hurt, never complained. Things that were too good to be true usually were.

The only surprise came toward the end of the time in the conference room, when Andrews asked, "What happens to the games Rotinom played in—are they forfeits?"

Collins looked to the lawyers, then to Andrews.

"No," he said. "They stand. Since this is unprecedented and since this, uh, situation is not bound by any contract with the players, we will treat this as a player who violated a league rule. He's out for future games, but the team will not be made to lose any victories."

Kelly moved up in his chair. "So the Stormcats remain 17-0 going into Sunday's game?" he clarified.

"That's correct," Collins said. And then, suddenly: "Which player gave you the chip?"

"I never said it was a player," Andrews said. She would be damned if she would reveal a source, though it was fairly obvious it probably was a player.

There was a brief silence, partly because Andrews was basically done, and because she was thinking what Gantriel would be dealing with: No first-string quarterback and no Rotinom on Sunday.

She cleared her throat and turned to Daugava.

"Doctor," she said, "we have heard why you got away with it, and how you pulled it off, but my question is why?"

"Miss Andrews," said Daugava, still composed and polite, "I worked for many years in a job I enjoyed, yes, but one that did not satisfy me. I was always under restrictions. Someone else's budget, someone else's timetable. You did a job based on the time given you, based on someone else's orders and, often, on their designs. If you thought you could improve those designs, well..." he shook his head slightly, "sometimes people don't listen. It is a blow to their ego.

"So I would go home at night and work on my own projects. It satisfied me. I could be creative. I could test something as long as I wanted. I had the time—I have no family and no other hobbies—so I worked. And I kept working. And it became a challenge. I decided early on football would be the best, physical test. It was."

"Did you ever think the plan would fail?" she asked.

Daugava smiled. "I had doubts early on, but that changed one day."

"What happened?" Andrews asked.

"I once heard two men in the diner talking about the day's previous game. One man turned to the other and said, 'Rotinom—he is not human. He's a machine!' I thought I had been found out. Then the man continued, saying Riga would be the MVP. I asked the man what 'MVP' meant, and he told me."

Daugava sat back in his chair and smiled. "So Miss Andrews, yes, the secret is out, but the truth is, now, now I am satisfied. My work prevailed."

Ego, Andrews thought. Daugava's ego just came wrapped in a polite package, but he was no different from the Scrantons of the world. It was all about him.

Collins spoke. "Anything more?"

Kelly looked at Andrews.

"Catharine?"

She shook her head no.

"We're good to go," he said. "Thanks for your candor, Commissioner."

He nodded at her then they all broke like a huddle, players spreading out to their positions. Scranton briskly made his way to his office, though since his suspension would be immediate it was more of an escape. Daugava walked slowly down the hallway to the exit, to go home to an almost empty apartment and a football player who would not play anymore. Collins and his lawyers left for their private jet downtown. Kelly headed for the airport to go back to New York.

"Great reporting," he said. "Call when you're done."

And Andrews headed home to write.

She wrote for hours, with no breaks, finally realizing that hunched tightness that came with the zone she got in when she was writing. A dull throbbing rose in her neck and shoulders when she sat for too long. She finished and stared at her screen.

Catharine Payton Andrews / The American / Cleveland: League officials admitted to an incredible, almost unbelievable scandal Friday: The Stormcats' Riga Rotinom is a machine, a robot created in a small apartment by a retired Cleveland engineer....

And so it went. She read it again and sent it to Kelly. This one would be "lawyered," a term meaning a story that a media company's attorneys also would edit. Kelly, having had a brief stint years earlier as a courts editor, said he did not foresee problems. He was right. The lawyers read it and got back to him immediately: Air tight. No changes.

In minutes, the comments field online would fill, her phone would ring with other reporters wanting to know about the story and how she got it. The few remaining television talk shows would immediately try to book her. At least three publishers would contact her for a book and movie deal.

Catharine wouldn't get the messages until the following morning. She had done something she never did right after she finished writing—she turned her PDR to mute. She poured herself a glass of wine and sat on the couch with Ginger.

"Movie night, G," she said. "Just you and me—no work."

CHAPTER 36

When Catharine woke the next morning, she turned on her PDR and it lit up like a Christmas tree. Everyone, it seemed, wanted something from her. Ginger nudged her to go out. News flashes popped up. At least she was being given credit in most of the rewritten stories by other media outlets. Her father, editor and several colleagues had called. By the time she was done answering even a fraction of the calls it was time to go to the stadium for the obligatory follow-up.

She needed to catch Gantriel to find who planned to play in Rotinom's place, and she wanted to grab some of the players. She found Trent and they split up the players they would go after.

Andrews hated the waiting game. There was a light practice only and players worked on various skills, work-outs and treatments, so she just had to catch them as she could. The media presence was extra heavy, as expected. She remembered sitting in her car waiting for Daugava at his apartment as she stared endlessly at the old brick building. It had all been worth it, she thought.

She got a few strange looks and an occasional hello as players sauntered by. She caught Carver near the parking lot, getting his reaction on Rotinom and learning what he expected from Atlanta's defense. Players all said the same thing: "Shocked," "too good to be true," "had no idea." All true. Rotinom went in, played hard, rarely spoke, and never hung out with anyone. No one knew him. Carver left, and Andrews spotted Canton.

"Tiger," she said, "hang on."

He stopped, looked around, and waited as she hustled over.

"Well," she said, "Big news is out today."

"Yeah," he said. "I read the story. It was fair."

"So's the game now," she said and then, lowering her voice: "Thanks for your help."

"No problem," he said quietly. "You never said in your story which player gave you the chip."

"I never said it was a player," she said, and they exchanged a look.

When Canton brought out the chip at Mary-Jo's that night, Andrews had been incredulous. She showed it to Madison Robinson and found out how advanced it was. Traditionally, on a story with an anonymous source, the reporter's editor is told who the source is. Not this time. That was the agreement; only she would know. So Canton and Andrews stood for a moment, neither saying a word as the light rain that had started to fall turned to wet snow.

"Any comment on how the defense will perform without Rotinom?" she asked.

"Yes," he said, "with heart."

And with that he stepped into the "Players Only" entrance to work out.

PART V

THE GAME

CHAPTER 37

By Sunday morning Clevelanders could hear the scrape and rumble of salt trucks and plows. As many as eight inches had fallen in some parts, with Emerald Lake Stadium blanketed. Crews were out immediately shoveling the sidelines and plowing the field, but the forecast called for continued snow all day.

The teams arrived early for their taping and stretching and light drills. The Stormcats' spirits had fallen with the snow the night before when Sails and his staff had called each player to let them know about Rotinom. Most also had calls from radio stations all over the country, television stations, publications, websites—everyone had picked up the story about Rotinom. But the number of credentialed reporters had stayed the same, since the story had just broken. So most of the media was kept at arm's-length outside the stadium. Television did their usual man-on-the-street questioning Cleveland fans, still stunned at the news. But the solace for fans came in the league's decision not to have Cleveland forfeit its games. The locker room turned into a bit of a haven. Cuya Aconttie sat stoically, getting his shoulder rubbed before the game. Carver stretched as tiny earpieces piped in music to his private world. Canton sat at his locker, not talking to anyone, his head hung, trying to concentrate on his defensive assignments. Occasionally, he felt a teammate's friendly pat against his shoulder pads.

Gantriel huddled in his office with his coaches. They had relied too much on Rotinom, but who wouldn't in his position? Run plays had moved more and more up the middle behind the big man, or machine as the case were. They had to run more swings to the outside with Carver. Thomas would still carry up the middle to balance things. Lanier Broda was one of the few people happy to see Rotinom gone, since it meant his old job back at center. And the survivor's guilt that sometimes came with playing because a teammate had been injured? Well, that just wasn't there for him. And it wasn't there for Aconttie, who had no time for anything except the game. When he was away from the stadium he studied the playbook. When he was at practice, it was taking snap after snap. Aconttie had one week to get up to speed, to lead a team in their biggest game all year. If he had a week to become an astronaut he would have felt more confident.

Atlanta's locker room contrasted Cleveland's; the players were jubilant and loose after hearing the Rotinom story. But the league and team had clammed up. No one close to it was saying a word. It had all come out in the conference room days earlier. So radio talkers were left to speculate and TV crews had been dispatched to interview people in lab coats who knew nothing about the story.

Gantriel gathered his troops for his pep talk. Men who played professional football were spoken to differently than college kids. They knew the score, they knew their job, they knew what had to be done. But that didn't lessen the need for Gantriel to make sure they were ready.

"Front and center!" boomed an assistant coach with the deepest and loudest voice.

Gantriel looked around, letting his eyes fall on the players nearest him until peace and quiet sifted over the room, the only peace the team would know the next few hours.

"Win," he said to the room in a gentle voice. "That's it, that's my message: Win." He waited a moment and saw the puzzled looks stare back.

"Listen," he said, again softly. "This is big, no doubt. And we're down a key player. You know what? I don't care. I really don't. Nothing to worry about since he isn't here and won't be here. We know what we've got to do. This isn't win-one-for-the-Gipper time, this is win one for yourselves. You didn't get here because of one player; you got here because of each other. You picked each other up all year. You buried opponents because you executed and you never, ever quit!"

Gantriel's fire inside slowly rose through him and burned its way out, reaching every man in the locker room. Heads nodded, some hands clapped in that dull, muffled sound that comes from wearing layers of wrapped tape.

"The coaches, we did what we did to help. But we're here in this position today for one reason and one reason only: YOU!"

More clapping, louder voices in agreement. Some of the players looked at one another. This definitely wasn't a "Win one for the Gipper" speech.

"You played hard, you kept your focus, you never let up. You feeling sorry we lost a couple of starters this week? That's the breaks, that's the game, things happen. You say you got a raw deal? Tough! Take it out on the guy across the line! (More clapping) Take it out by running faster! (Louder voices) By hitting harder! (Cheers) This is your game! This is your game! This is your game! WIN! WIN! WIN!"

Gantriel, always reserved, had worked himself into a rare frenzy. Now, his team was ready. He forgot to tell them that no matter what happened today, they would remember this for the rest of their lives.

By the time the Cleveland and Atlanta captains met at midfield in Emerald Lake Stadium, snow continued to fall smoothly. The peace of the quiet, steady falling snow contrasted how each and every Stormcat felt: Like hungry animals, in a pack, ready to do what they had to do to survive.

Players huddled closely around the coaches, and Canton drew them in tight. "Here we go, here we go!" His succinct message boomed out as one word: "SIXTYMINUTESWIN!" Players yelled, clapped, grunted.

They took the field.

Kenny Studen stood, jumping on his own goal line, partly because of nerves but mostly to stay warm. He used to stand with Aconttie, who returned kicks, but not today. No way would the team take a chance on its fourth-string quarterback getting hurt returning a kick.

The Atlanta kicker boomed it, long and end over end, but not quite as far as he wanted. Studen had decided: If it were in the end zone he would down it. But this kick wasn't going to reach the end zone. The swirly gusts inside the stadium held it up just enough so that he caught it on his own 2-yard line, and he took off. He knew his blockers would be to his left, so he raced for the sideline. Defenders thundered at him, falling like soldiers in battle behind his blockers. When three defenders broke down the sideline and hungrily ran for him, he instinctively cut to his right, back to midfield. He tore through an opening and shot up the middle of the field, juked a defender at the 35, skirted around another at the 50, and he was still on his feet past midfield. Studen kept his stride, outrunning the defense, and no one touched him the rest of the way. He flipped the ball to the referee and turned to look for flags. When a player changes direction on his own, the free-lancing often brings a flag—a clip, a bad block. When the action on the field suddenly shifts, it often catches offensive players in the unenviable position of having to block defenders in the other direction, and sometimes against their backs. But it didn't happen. The game was only seconds old, and the Stormcats were up 6-0.

If Gantriel's speech weren't enough for motivation, then the runback was. The sidelines and stadium exploded as Gantriel stood with Aconttie and yelled out the play for the two-point conversion.

"Gun spread, two-hole draw!" "Gun spread, two-hole draw—you got that?!" Gantriel shouted, shoving his quarterback onto the field. It wasn't the mini-pep talk he had in mind for Aconttie, but it would have to do. Instead of having to charge up Aconttie for a series of plays, the coach just needed one play. And Aconttie knew it. The "two-hole" indicated where in the offensive line the play would go. Aconttie went in and calmly called the formation. Then, standing a few feet behind his center, with two receivers on each end of the scrimmage line and the defense scrambling, he took the snap. He waited a split-second as he looked at his receivers in the end zone—and handed off to Thomas. The fullback took the ball, angling a bit to his right, and plowed in untouched. The defense crunched in on him, but seconds later the green light lit up like a traffic signal on the "goal-line-stand" clock. Two points. Cleveland 8, Atlanta 0.

Polsky, Cleveland's kicker, pounded the ball into the end zone, and Atlanta took the field. The first play was a safe one, a run up the middle. The defensive line slowed the running back, and Canton dug in and hit him head-on, driving him down into the snow. The crowd came to life, and teammates congratulated Canton. He knew it was one play, but it was the start he and the defense needed. He loved playing in a big game, with something on the line. And he loved the first hit. But the thing he realized he hadn't had all season was a pat on the back, a thumb's up—any positive sign from Rotinom. The big man would walk back to his position and get set for the next play.

Atlanta then tried a pitchout to the running back, good for 7 yards. Third and one, the defense needed to tighten. The quarterback faked to his fullback, took a step back, and fired to a streaking receiver down the right sideline. He caught it in stride, and if it weren't for a safety coming over to help he would have scored. The gain of more than 20 put the ball inside Cleveland territory.

Atlanta's quarterback, a sandy-haired Californian named Steve Noble, looked over the defense and sent his receivers wide, lined up near each sideline.

"Hut, hut, HUT!" he yelled, and faded to pass. Canton pulled back. Then, all of a sudden, Noble shoveled an end-over-end pass to Bill Williams, the Atlanta running back, who caught the ball as he hurdled through the line. Canton was too far back and could only lunge at Williams as he raced easily into the end zone. Canton picked himself off the ground to see the tiny green light flash on the referee's receiver, another indication from the microchip noting the ball had crossed the goal line. The extra point brought the game to within one, 8-7.

This time, before the Stormcats took the field after the kickoff, Gantriel turned to Aconttie.

"You ready? You ready to go?" he said, as calmly as he could contain himself. "This is your team now; drive them." Aconttie didn't say a word. He nodded and trotted onto the field.

In the huddle he saw the faces who looked to him now not as the guy who spent most of his time on the sidelines, holding a clipboard charting plays, but as a leader. This wasn't a democracy. He was thrust into the role, and it was his job, and there was no time to whine about it.

"Pro set, counter toss 8, on three, ready, break!" Aconttie boomed the play. The call was for Carver to take a pitchout on first down and get around the right side. But the Atlanta defense read it and he barely gained a yard. Thomas fared no better through the middle on the next play, and an Aconttie pass on third down fell incomplete. The Stormcats had to punt. Not too fantastic of a start for Aconttie and the offense.

When Canton trotted back on the field, he vowed not to be fooled again, like the touchdown minutes earlier. He stretched out his hands, puffs of breath shooting through his facemask, as he waited for Noble to call the play. The Atlanta quarterback dropped back three steps and threw directly to a receiver down the sidelines. First down inside Stormcat territory.

"Damnit," muttered Canton to no one as the teams moved downfield. Atlanta was playing with no fear, doing whatever they wanted against the Cleveland defense.

Then Williams established himself. The agile running back danced and scampered his way through the defense, needing only one block and turning it into gains of 6, 7, 8 yards. First downs came easily. On a second-down play, Williams took a handoff and cut seriously to his left for a 13-yard gain to the Stormcat 19. Groans across the stadium drowned any cheers or boos.

In the quick defensive huddle, Canton turned to his teammates and said, "Stops—right here, right now." But as he looked into the eyes of the line of players, he could see a fire was gone. Rotinom wasn't missed in the locker room, but he was missed on the field. No way Williams would be running over the defense, no way Noble would have time to throw. They knew it.

Noble brought his team to the line, faked to the fullback and threw a short pass to Williams, who gained 4 before being pushed out of bounds. When Canton saw the big fullback line up behind Noble, he knew the next play was going to him. They would try to grind it out the rest of the way. Canton cheated in a bit and then, after a split-second delay, charged toward the line from his linebacker position. The fullback took the handoff, and bulled his way into the line. But Canton met him with a head of steam and plowed him backward. Loss of 2.

It was the spark Cleveland needed.

"Watch the corner!" Canton yelled at his defense. It was his team, no matter how good Rotinom had been all year. And on third-and-7 that's exactly what Noble wanted to do—throw down the sidelines. But a Cleveland defensive back leaped and tipped the ball away from the outstretched arms of the receiver. Atlanta settled for a field goal and took a 10-8 lead.

It's funny how football scores work. The scoreboard showed Atlanta taking the lead, but both coaches knew the momentum on the last series of plays belonged to Cleveland. The Stormcats had won the battle over the last few minutes, keeping Atlanta out of the end zone and forcing a field goal. Letting up three points is always better than giving six.

The first half continued. Cleveland's defense kept stopping Atlanta, forcing punts. Aconttie did his best trying to lead Cleveland's offense, but could not get on track. The athlete in him kept trying, but the lack of game experience at quarterback had hurt. Except for a late pass to LeBon, the Stormcat quarterback could not manage much against the Atlanta defense. Carver slowly found his groove, and Thomas managed a few yards on the ground, but the Stormcats had not been able to get back in the red zone—that magical area past the opponent's 20-yard line—the rest of the half. Their breath pulsing between the bars of their face masks, the players trudged to their respective locker rooms at the sound of the gun. Fans huddled to stay warm beneath ponchos as the snow kept coming and the temperature stayed below freezing. People stared at the giant scoreboard—not because they didn't know the score, but because it showed something no one had seen all year: It was the first time Cleveland had been behind going into the third quarter.

The announcers were almost giddy, pointing it out. The fans couldn't hear them, but no matter. They knew the dominant team they followed all year was different.

In the locker room, coaches divvied up their players and went over what was working, what wasn't. Towels and water cups already covered the carpet. Helmets thudded on the ground as players caught their breath.

Aconttie and the offensive coaches huddled over plays, the coaches showing more patience than usual. Other than preseason games, it wasn't often a fourth-string quarterback was relied on to lead the team.

A clubhouse worker keeping track of the time knocked on Gantriel's door, letting him know it was almost time to go back on the field. Gantriel gathered his troops. There was so much to yell about, so much to say, but he wanted this to be quick. He knew his troops were pushing out there.

"We go in five," he said, "so listen up."

Tired heads turned.

"I know you're going hard, I know you're trying to make things happen. You've got to dig, dig inside for more, find it, and push these bastards out. They came into your house, and they don't want to just beat you; they want to knock you out."

He saw faces nodding.

"When they push you, push back harder. Put 'em in the dirt! Make 'em eat snow! CRUSH THEM!"

And the cries started, like a high school team's frenzy against an arch-rival, and they made for the double-doorway that led to the tunnel that opened up to the field.

Atlanta's quarterback started the second half the way he had the first—controlling the ball, establishing a running game with Williams, then long passes to get into field-goal range. But Canton had had enough. On a second down, he called for the defense to blitz. He raced through the line, sidestepped a running back and lunged at Noble, who grunted as Canton hit him. The two fell as one. But the linebacker's tackle was too late. The quarterback got the pass off, his receiver leaping and making the catch over the middle.

Canton didn't say anything. He picked himself up, got back to his teammates, and looked them in the eyes. Snow caked in creases on his jersey. He turned around for a moment and looked at Noble in the huddle as he remembered studying Atlanta's offense all week on paper. In a situation like this, they sometimes would go back to the pass to catch a defense off guard when they got close to the opponent's 20-yard line.

"Do it again," he said, turning back to his teammates.

The defense followed Canton, they always did, even at crazier moments like this. Canton may not have been the MVP of the team all year, but his teammates listened to him.

Noble lined up under center, and Canton inched closer, but not too much. He didn't want to give away the fact the defense was going to rush again.

"Blue! Forty-eight!" Noble cried. "Blue! Forty-eight!"

At Noble's command, a receiver started to move to a new position on the line of scrimmage. Canton crept in slowly as a defensive back followed the receiver.

"Set, hut…hut…"

Canton moved even closer to the line.

"HUT!"

The defensive back also had crept up, gambling on the blitz. He and Canton banged through, angling for a surprised Noble who quickly tried to set and throw, but Canton crashed through and plowed into him. Noble didn't have time to cover the ball, which spilled out and bounced along. Players scrambled to pounce on it as it slipped through their fingers and bounced back even further. Finally, a scrum ensued: An Atlanta player and a Cleveland player each dived, landing on the ball and then drawing their teammates on top. They looked like a pack of dogs going after dinner. Players pulled back fingers—any fingers—that were grasping the ball. Sometimes it was a teammate's. It didn't matter; they just needed the football. The officials finally made it to the pile and peeled off the players one by one. A referee looked at the mess, stood tall and pointed in the opposite way Atlanta was trying to move.

The crowd bellowed when the officials confirmed it was Cleveland's ball. Noble looked up and sighed. Canton ran off the field, fortified with a few back-slaps from teammates amid the roar of the fans, and was met by more congratulatory pats from his coaches.

Gantriel turned to Aconttie, who stayed as close to his coach as possible.

"Now, now you roll," Gantriel said. "Start with the runs, go to the passes, work it downfield. You're up on the plays, we're ready, move the ball!"

Aconttie nodded and headed to the field. Yeah, he thought, I'm up on the plays, mindlessly patting the laminated cheat sheet attached to his wrist.

His first call was a simple run play for Carver off tackle to the left. Carver was crushed as he hit the line of scrimmage.

"Damn it!" Aconttie said back in the huddle. "We're gonna do that one again. Same play—except this time we're gonna block for RC!"

A voice started to speak, but Aconttie cut him off.

"I know, I know," he said, anticipating the question. "But we're going again."

It was rare for the exact call to be repeated on consecutive plays. And it broke from Gantriel's game plan. But Aconttie figured it was the last thing Atlanta would look for, and he needed a spark.

He walked to his position behind center and barked out the signals. Thomas and Carver bent, frozen in the backfield, snow still falling. Aconttie took the snap, turned and shoved it into Carver's gut. The running back took two steps before cutting his way sharply to his left and seeing Brock McAdams level his defender. Carver stepped through a hole big enough for two of him and sliced his way past a linebacker for the first down. He was in open field, slowed a bit on the snow, but then again so was the defense. He tucked away the ball as he sprinted for the sideline. He crossed midfield untouched until a cornerback ended the play with an open-field tackle. For the second time in minutes, the crowd roared. The Stormcats were in Atlanta territory, all because of Aconttie's call and Carver's running and an offensive line that pushed the Atlanta defense—teamwork.

The Stormcats gathered between two once-cleared yard lines. Snow fell so fast it covered the many footprints scattered in all directions. The team of officials would have blended in were it not for their black stripes and gloves. Carver stood a minute, catching his breath, watching it. Having been raised in Iowa, he was used to snow, which seemed to cover the fields near his home for months at a time before melting. Single strands of once-plowed stalks poked out of the permafrost. In his home state, you grew quickly to embrace snow, knowing it would always be there at certain times of the year, or to hate it. He always loved it.

Aconttie and his teammates, feeling a resurgence, walked to the line of scrimmage with a purpose. The young quarterback glared at the defense. He threw on first down over the middle to Wisgenti, who gained 18 yards to the Atlanta 33. He handed off to Thomas, who banged forward for 5 yards to the 28 but followed it with an incomplete pass intended for LeBon. On third-and-5 he was tempted to call a timeout but changed his mind. He faced the defense, took three steps back, and fired quickly to a running Culpepper on the right. The big Georgian was running an arrow route, straight and fast on a slant to the sidelines. Aconttie fired the ball, and Culpepper leaped, felt his fingertips touch the ball—and then felt that empty feeling seeing it bounce away.

Aconttie tugged at his face mask, a habit he picked up in high school. He looked to the sidelines, and Gantriel's order was clear when he saw several players jogging at him: We're kicking. He trotted off and touched Polsky on his helmet for good luck.

The kick was good, and the crowd muffled claps with mittens and gloves. The scoreboard flashed 11-10 with less than 10 minutes left in the third quarter.

The teams traded punts after that, both threatening for a while until a receiver dropped the ball or a running back slipped. Weather was becoming the third team in this game, and Mother Nature was badgering Atlanta and Cleveland equally. The clock slipped into the final quarter as Cleveland mounted a drive, which again forced Aconttie into a third-down play. He brought his team to the line, called the snap, and faded. Atlanta blitzed. He should have known, but he was forced to scramble. He was hoping to hit LeBon or Wisgenti in the middle or left, but he ran to his right to escape the horde chasing him. Gantriel insisted every pass play have a safety option, a receiver who ran a pattern to a certain part of the field in the event the quarterback had to change direction—like in the case of a blitz. And that's exactly what Culpepper had done. He was at the right sideline when Aconttie spotted him, the ball thrown his way.

The defense didn't stop when Aconttie threw. A defender collapsed on him, sending Aconttie straight down, his throwing shoulder thudding on the ground, a mixture of snow and grass lodging in his face mask. Aconttie didn't see Culpepper catch it, but the cheering was all he needed. That's really what replays were for—quarterbacks who ended up taking a licking on key pass plays.

Aconttie strode to the line and kept directing his team.

Insurance points here would be key. One point was too slim of a margin; Cleveland needed to score. Thomas pushed his way into the line for 6 yards, Carver scampered off tackle for 8 more. Carver caught a pass in the flat and gained 7 behind good blocking. The Stormcats and the clock kept moving. They got the ball down to the 33 when Aconttie saw the sideline wanting a timeout. He turned to the nearest referee.

"Time, ref," Aconttie said and trotted to Gantriel.

"We need three," was Gantriel's greeting to his quarterback. "And no more timeouts, we're done," he said, reminding his quarterback that the team had used its allotment.

Aconttie looked at his coach, sipping a water bottle someone had handed him.

"We're on the 33. That's a 47-yard kick. I need it closer, Cuya. With this wind, we have to get closer."

Aconttie nodded and offered up a play—a fake pass, then a run. Gantriel did not agree. He gave Aconttie the play.

"Keep it up, QB, keep 'em moving," Gantriel said as he patted his shoulder pads and sent him back into battle.

Aconttie lined up under center, took the snap, and turned to give a fake to Carver. But he slipped on the slushy mix that was starting to freeze and went down, the ball skidding behind him. Atlanta pounced, gathering it in on their own 40. A clump of defenders surrounded their teammate who had recovered the ball and escorted him to the sidelines.

Aconttie tugged off his chinstrap and trotted to the sideline as the defense trudged back on.

Canton's squad would have to be vigilant. If they allowed 30 or 35 yards, Atlanta would be in field-goal range. With the clock running in the final quarter, Canton figured Atlanta would run, run, run. And that's exactly what they did. Williams left on first down, Williams right on second down. A fake pass, then a quick handoff to Williams on third, and he gained the first. But on first down the Atlanta quarterback handed off to his fullback—probably to give Williams a quick breather—and Cleveland's defense pounded him, keeping him upright behind the line of scrimmage, until the ball popped out. Canton scrambled, landed on it, then it came loose again. It bounced backward as Noble tried to scoop it up; it slipped through his hands. Finally a Cleveland defender landed on it, pulled it in like it was the most valuable thing he had ever touched, and cradled it until the refs blew the play dead. Atlanta's gains on the three previous plays were wiped out. Cleveland had the ball back around midfield. The residue of weather is turnovers, and they had crept into this game.

Again, Aconttie trudged to the line, not letting his brain remind himself how tired his body was.

Sometimes plays come together nicely. The line blocks, the defense doesn't blitz, the receiver gets open. First down was one of those plays. Aconttie hit Wisgenti across the middle, and the agile receiver took it in stride, stiff-armed a defender and turned upfield before being brought down at the 36. The defense was sure the ball would be handed to Carver, so Aconttie did the opposite. He gave it to Thomas, and the big fullback bulled his way for 4 yards to the 32. Aconttie then called his own number and snuck around the right side for a gain of 4 more. On third-and-2 he sent three receivers deep—then threw a short pass to Carver, who gained 5 yards.

Coaches often don't care for kickers that much. They had two jobs—kick the ball through the uprights, or kick the ball downfield. Coaches preferred the six points to the three anytime, obviously. But Gantriel had no qualms sending Polsky onto the field. Aconttie and Polsky knelt quietly, neither saying a word as they cleared a spot in the snow where the ball would land. After tacking on yards for the goal posts and for the spot where the ball would be placed, it would amount to a 40-yard kick. Gantriel always thought of these extra yards as "taxes."

The crowd hushed as they waited for the snap. Players froze on the sidelines. The officials watched. The one person in the stadium who wasn't nervous was Polsky. He had been paying attention to the wind all day, and in Cleveland's home stadium, wind was a funny thing. It didn't move in a nice, neat pattern; it swirled and whipped, directionless, like a drunken dancer in a club after midnight. But right now it was blowing through the goal posts that Polsky stared at.

Atlanta didn't even call a timeout to try to rattle Polsky. The snap came, and Polsky's kick cleared the crossbar with a few feet to spare. Cleveland took a three-point lead, 14-10.

On the kickoff, Polsky boomed the ball into the end zone but, surprisingly, the Atlanta returner didn't down it. He ran it out. He turned on the speed immediately, seemingly the only player who could move in the snow. He didn't angle for the sidelines; instead, he shot his way upfield, mystifying the Cleveland defenders. He got all the way to the Cleveland 20 before being brought down in a leaping, ankle tackle.

The collective groan from the stands sounded like a long disappointing moan. After Cleveland's field goal, there were six minutes remaining—time for one drive for Atlanta to go downfield. But now, those six minutes might as well have been six hours. All they needed was 20 short yards. Forget a field goal; they wanted six now.

Noble blew into his hands, then approached the line.

"Orange! Orange!" he yelled, his receivers going in motion.

He faked the ball to Williams, who escaped through the line and turned back. Noble tossed the ball lightly over defenders' hands right to Williams, who turned and juked his way upfield before Canton tackled him at the 9. On the next play Williams took a handoff and was hit at the line of scrimmage. Atlanta was in no hurry. The offense could taste a touchdown they were so close. Linemen rose slowly as the clock kept moving. Williams managed two more and got down to the 7. Noble then took the ball himself and ran it in, the extra point was good, and Atlanta was up, 17-14.

McAdams hadn't said much all game. Partly because he was tired, partly because he didn't say much during games. But he found his quarterback next to Thomas and Carver and stuck his paw between them.

Thomas looked at Aconttie. The quarterback glanced at Carver. Then they all looked at McAdams.

"Score," the big lineman said. "This drive. Run up over my freakin' back if you want. But let's score."

Thomas tapped McAdams' hand. Carver put his atop his teammates. "Far out" was all Aconttie could say as he put his on top of the three.

With that McAdams hit his own helmet a few times and huffed off.

"Far out," Aconttie said again, watching the lineman as he hulked his way to the sideline, ready to hit the field again.

"Was that a pep talk from McAdams?" asked Carver.

"Yeah," Thomas said. "I almost wished Wisgenti was over here with one of his puns."

The ice-breaker was quick but needed.

After the kickoff, which Cleveland downed in the end zone, the Stormcats' chances came down to 3:59. Time for one drive to score. Gantriel had to make his calculations quickly, looking at the field: Go for the tie, or the win. He had to think of time remaining, how tired his defense was, and the weather conditions.

Gantriel looked at the clock and saw a lot of time. Of course, if the Stormcats had been ahead, the same time would have looked like very little to the coach. It was always a wishful reflection on his part, the inner battle he had with time every game.

The offense had trotted onto the field, but Aconttie stood back for a second, next to his coach. He no longer was the young quarterback with no experience. He had aged in this game, and was leading his team. And they were following.

Gantriel looked at him: "Get in the end zone," he said, as a smile crept across Aconttie's face. He snapped his chin strap and ran to meet his offense.

"OK, boys, we roll now," he said. "Let's get the six." Eyes widened as they looked up, but no one said a word. Aconttie called a draw, and followed it with a short pass to the flat. "Ready, break!" Aconttie broke the huddle and moved to the line.

With Wisgenti and LeBon lined on one side and Culpepper on the other, Aconttie faded to pass, stood, looked, danced for a moment in place—and handed the ball to Carver. The defense, busy covering receivers downfield, scrambled to tackle Carver, who raced his way for 14 yards before dancing out of bounds to stop the clock. The Stormcats quickly moved to the line of scrimmage, with receivers lining up wide left and right. They each had specific routes to run, all for one purpose: To decoy the defense away from

Aconttie and Thomas. The quarterback looked downfield for a moment and then flipped a quick throw to the lumbering fullback, who stayed inbounds long enough to put his shoulder into one defender before being pushed out of bounds near his own sideline. Pats on the back quickly energized him to hustle back into the huddle after a 4-yard gain.

Cleveland was nearing midfield. Aconttie hit Culpepper on first down, then LeBon on second. They pushed into Atlanta territory. Aconttie looked at the tired faces in the huddle. No one was looking at him. Everyone had their heads down, breath pushing out between face masks like a circle of snorting bulls.

"Suck it up, let's keep going. Red 300-30, on two, ready break!"

The Atlanta defense, also tired, crept to the line of scrimmage. Aconttie moved cautiously. The defense was playing run all the way. The teams neared a two-minute warning, which would earn them a breather and Aconttie a quick talk from Gantriel. Aconttie had called for a handoff to Carver after fading back three steps, but he didn't like the defense. He might as well have told them what he was going to call, they had moved in so close. By the time he handed the ball to Carver the defenders would have caved in on the running back. Carver would have been lucky to get up to the line of scrimmage.

"April clock! April clock!" Aconttie screamed. "April" was the coded word of the quarter—Gantriel made sure to change the code every quarter so a defense couldn't figure out when Aconttie was changing the play. If Aconttie yelled any month of the year, he would change the play. But when he yelled "clock" that added yet another dimension: He would try to draw the defense offsides.

"Hut, hut, hut…HUTHUT!" Suddenly, three defenders jumped across, a flag flew, and referees' hands went up. Aconttie turned and couldn't help from smiling. They had gained 5 yards on the penalty and stopped the clock.

It was a ploy that couldn't be used often, and they hadn't called it all game, but it worked now, when it was needed.

Aconttie took the snap and handed it to Carver, who cradled it in and ran around the left side. Daylight, he just needed a bit of daylight, and he found it right before the sidelines. He turned upfield before three defenders crashed into him at the 39. The officials signaled the two-minute warning, and everyone took their breaks.

"Look at them," LeBon said to his receiver mate, Wisgenti.

"Who?"

"The fans. You can almost hear their prayers. They are asking God for us to win. I think God has bigger things on his mind than a football game in the snow in Cleveland."

"You don't know that," Wisgenti said. "No other games on right now. If I were in the stands I'd be praying, too."

LeBon smiled. Wisgenti always had a glib comment no matter the occasion. He was all business running his routes and he always stayed prepared, but most other times he could keep things loose.

Television went to commercial, Aconttie went to the sidelines, but fans just stood. Like LeBon guessed, many were praying. It was a part of them, generation after generation. This year had been different. No game had been this close for Cleveland all season, no game this exciting. The Stormcats always had a healthy lead by this time. Now they were in a dogfight. And amazingly, their No. 4 quarterback was leading the way.

McAdams walked to the sidelines and bypassed the bench, the water table and the medical tent. He walked over to the crowd and started to scream "Let's go Storm-cats!" and then clapping his hands.

The fans in front at first didn't hear him. So he repeated himself.

"Let's go Storm-cats!"

The crowd picked it up. At first it was a few rows, and then the vocal wave rushed through the section, and then another, and within seconds anyone in the crowd had forgotten their prayers and put down their beers and started yelling in unison.

"Let's go Storm-cats! Let's go Storm-cats!"

About the only people on the Cleveland sidelines who didn't look up at the crowd were Gantriel and Aconttie. They stood, inches from each other. The quarterback squirted a water bottle into his mouth.

"Good change," he said about drawing the defense offsides. "Time enough," he said. "Time enough now. Now, here's what we do…"

A whistle blew, ending the mini-lesson.

Aconttie pulled up behind center and yelled his signals.

He faded and looked, looked, looked, nobody was open. He scrambled to his right, then circled back to his left as he threw the ball in the general direction of Wisgenti but nowhere close enough for the lanky receiver to catch. It sailed out of bounds and bounced into the Stormcat bench. The clock stopped momentarily. Get open, Aconttie thought as he lined up for second down. But as he crouched behind his center he saw only four linemen; Atlanta had most of their defense back to defend the pass. Aconttie took the snap, faded, and saw what he expected to see: All his receivers were covered. So he ran. He took off toward the sidelines, flashing a quick glance to the upright red marker showing where the first down was. Snow kicked up from his cleats as he tried to cut in to the earth. He saw a defender coming at him as he raced down the sidelines. Stepping out meant the clock would stop; he had the first down. But he couldn't do it. It was yardage, every step getting them closer to the goal. He ran and saw a red jersey angling at him from the left. Aconttie ran on, he felt the reach of the defender, a stretched hand pleading for a tackle, he kept moving forward, churning his legs.

Muscle memory kicked in, and Aconttie instinctively remembered an old schoolyard trick he had done once on a muddy field.

He simply stopped.

He had put on the brakes, completely, which was a challenge in the snow. And when he did the defender flew by, skidding in the snow, as Aconttie stood for no more than half a second. Then he started running again. The stop-start move bought him more yards, but it gave defenders behind him time to catch up. Still, it was a brilliant maneuver, and he was down to the 19 before being pushed out of bounds.

The crowd cheered as he ran back to the huddle, his adrenalin surging.

"Nice," a tired teammate said.

"He looked bad," McAdams huffed.

"Highlight reel just got really good," LeBon said.

Aconttie ignored the compliments, called the play, and clapped his hands with new energy.

The clock ticked under a minute as a screen went to Carver, who swung around the weak side for 6 yards.

Aconttie had done a masterful job mixing up plays, and this one again caught the defense napping. The 'Cats could almost taste the end zone. No one was thinking field goal. But as Carver picked himself up and turned around he noticed the yellow flag near the line of scrimmage. His eyes were drawn to it, and he groaned.

The referee was already turning on his broadcasting unit. "Holding, offense, number 63..."

They regrouped in the huddle after losing the 5 yards. This time, it was Carver as the decoy and Thomas rushing, but the defense pounded him for a loss of 2. Cleveland was doing a good job of moving in the wrong direction. They were in Atlanta territory, and the wind in the stadium picked up. It whipped crazily. A kick, even from this distance, could be challenging. On second down, Aconttie pitched to Carver. But as he turned to toss the ball in that gentle, underhanded pitch they had worked on so many times in drills, Aconttie's feet went down. The snow packed in his cleats wasn't helping his traction, and the ball bounced over and behind Carver, who turned and scrambled for it. The defense rushed through, like clumsy dogs going after a piece of meat. Carver ran and scooped it up as a defender tackled him from behind. It was a huge loss. Aconttie frantically tried to get his team lined up as the referee set the ball on the Atlanta 41.

Aconttie looked at the clock: 17 seconds and counting. He turned to his teammates, who were scrambling to get to the line of scrimmage. Sixteen seconds. He looked left and barked out the snap count "Hut!" Fifteen seconds. "Hut!" The ball came to him as he faded, faked to his right quickly, and threw to Wisgenti on the left, who had shaken free of his defender to catch the ball as he was going out of bounds for the first down.

The clock wasn't the only thing stopped. The referees were huddling together, a yellow flag at their feet. Players tried to creep near them, to hear the call.

"Pass interference, offense, number 89..."

Wisgenti's eyes went wide as teammates rushed to hold him away from the officials. The Cleveland offensive coordinator threw his headset and screamed at the referees.

"Chicken-shit call! What the hell is that!?" Francis said when an official came near.

"Eighty-nine pushed the defender when he cut back, coach," the referee said sternly, as one of his brethren walked off the penalty, pushing Cleveland back even further.

That was that. The judge and jury on a football field rarely lost an argument, despite the yelling and protesting and even reviewing. The clock showed 12 seconds. Gantriel and his coaches signaled the final play.

Aconttie yelled at his teammates in the huddle, "Gun trips right Stooges max on three—everyone got that?" He looked around at alert faces, breath like smoke in the winter air, eyes widened at the call.

The wind had subsided some, for now, but the snow kept coming. The field was a mess, with cleat marks making it look like it had been tilled by a tractor. "Gun trips right Stooges max on three," Aconttie repeated sternly, then put his hand out, "for the six, gentlemen, ready, break!"

The offensive line moved toward their positions, anchors digging in for one final play, one more chance. Culpepper, LeBon and Wisgenti lined up on the right side, in a row, all poised and looking at Aconttie. The receivers were the three Stooges, in this play. When their name was called, they knew what routes had to be run and what had to be done.

Carver was off the field, and Thomas was the lone back. But for this final play he would not be touching the ball; his role was that of every man on the line—bodyguard. Maximum protection. The Stormcats had one chance at the end zone, and everyone in the stadium knew it would be a long pass. It was fourth and almost 40, but there would be no first down. It was get in the end zone on this play, or lose. By the time Aconttie faded and threw, the ball would have to be in the air about 50 yards. Not the longest pass he had ever thrown but a pretty good toss on any day.

Aconttie never bothered to move under center. He remained in shotgun, putting several feet between him and the offensive line.

"Hut…" The ball spiraled toward him as the defense surged. The line held. McAdams curled his hands into fists, forced himself not to grab or hold, and pushed forward with all the strength he could muster, keeping his man away from Aconttie, surging at him like he was a tackling dummy. The quarterback moved to his right, nearly slipping again in the snow, then regained his footing. Red jerseys began caving in toward him as he watched his receivers streak downfield in what looked like a track meet. He set, and heaved the ball downfield, a red jersey smacking into him and knocking him backward, then landing on him, crushing him into the snow.

The trio running downfield was not alone. A referee watched as the receivers and the defenders jockeyed for position, lightly dancing in place as the ball came near them on the 8-yard line. All looked up as the ball sailed toward the pack that had swarmed to this one place, the most important piece of the field. They leaped, as if in choreographed unison, as the ball fell toward them. But it was

Culpepper who jumped like he had never jumped before, tipping the ball backward with his left palm. His right arm was caught between two players. A defender jumped too late to catch the ball and crashed into the pack, knocking down most of the players, including Wisgenti, human bowling pins. The ball floated backward, toward the end zone and away from the pack.

Most of the pack.

LeBon was alone at the 3-yard line as the ball fell into his hands. He pulled it in and clutched it against his face mask as he pulled backward for a couple of steps and fell into the end zone. A nearby official put both hands in the air, signaling a touchdown as the microchip broke the plane, and he was followed by a second official motioning the same. No flags.

Wisgenti and Culpepper were the first to greet LeBon. They scooped themselves up from the pile of bodies and jumped on him in the end zone, screaming nothing coherent—just jubilation.

Aconttie had heard the crowd noise as he scrambled to his feet and raced downfield, passing his lumbering offensive linemen who he hugged along the way. The crowd had erupted as the scoreboard flashed a giant UNDEFEATED sign over the score line: Cleveland 20, Atlanta 17.

Gantriel's team made a beeline from the sidelines to the end zone as the coach turned to the benches and sat. His staff stood. But his own mental and physical exhaustion took over, and he plopped down. A photographer would capture the moment in what would become a Pulitzer Prize-winning photograph, the coach left alone as players ran onto the field.

Canton was first off the sidelines. Aconttie reached his teammates and leaped, being caught amid the screams and cheers and joy and hugs. Carver raced to the end zone and fell to his knees, looking to the sky, then fell backward and lay down. Even the stoic Thomas had run out, grabbed Polsky and lifted him like a sack over his shoulder. The crowd stood and cheered, as if they could call for an encore. That chance would come later, in the playoffs. For now, it was a celebration, players who had proved all day they belonged without their supposed one-man team, their game changer. They had found their collective heart.

And the snow kept coming, erasing the tracks on the field where Carver had run. Where Aconttie had scrambled and had been forced into a hero's role. Where the receiving corps had raced, where Canton had tackled and played the game he loved. Where the Stormcats had battled, and won.

EPILOGUE

Brooks Scranton, true to form, didn't come into the locker room. This time, though, it wasn't by choice. Collins and the league's board of directors quickly voted to remove him as team owner. He watched, stunned and happy, from home. It was different for him now. The league also took away a draft pick and slammed Scranton in the wallet with a massive fine, one of the largest ever, before removing him. He was out of a job and would have to find new creative pursuits somewhere, either in the financial world or sports, if that were possible. For now, he could only watch the playoffs from his home.

With a few injuries reported, Catharine Andrews had to prepare for the playoffs. She would continue to follow the Stormcats on their run through the postseason. Book publishers, agents and a movie studio kept approaching her about telling her story, and she told them all she would consider their offers—after the playoffs. Now, she had a job to do. But she told everyone she would not reveal who her source was, ever. Her reputation was everything to her. All the attention really didn't mean that much. She had just done her job.

Although one day, as she was going to take Ginger for a walk, an envelope appeared in her mailbox. No return address. She tore it open and read the brief note inside.

"Good reporting."

It was signed:

"Always for the Stormcats"

For some reason, the letter writer had underlined the first "T" and the "C" in "Stormcats."

Catharine smiled, put the note in her pocket, and tugged gently on the leash.

"Let's go, Ginger."

The Players Exchange—the stock index for fans—was suspended, briefly, to determine what to do with revenue gained from a fraudulent action. In the end, though, it was determined nothing could be done, and those who made money off their investments in Rotinom could keep their earnings.

Writers would be split over whether Tiger Canton deserved to be voted onto the all-NPL team. Some argued he was a leader who had a great season and was a catalyst in the Stormcats' undefeated season. Others, less informed, said he was simply riding Rotinom's shirttails. In the end, it was a close vote, and he got in. Andrews had no problem voting for him.

Janis Daugava didn't pay attention to the remaining schedule. He was getting ready to begin the emotional burden of dismantling his creation when the phone rang. He had not brought himself to take apart Rotinom, and while he knew he had to, it was not a job he relished. There would be other projects, he felt, but this one was special and they had accomplished so much.

"Dr. Daugava?" a voice said.

"Yes, this is he," the doctor replied cautiously.

"This is Nevada Collins."

Daugava was quiet for a moment, not knowing what

to expect. For his scheme—and that's what it was—he had dealt solely with Scranton. They both realized the fewer the people who knew about their plan, the fewer red flags would be raised. Not that any of that mattered now.

"Am I in some sort of trouble?" Daugava asked.

"No," the commissioner replied. "After the interview with Andrews, we never really spoke. I wanted to reach out to you. That was quite a... stunt you pulled off. Elaborate and scientific, but a stunt nonetheless."

"It was not my intention to create a spectacle," Daugava said, his voice not as deep as Collins' but just as authoritative.

"And it's not mine to admonish you now," Collins replied. "I understand you are not much of a football fan."

"No," Daugava said. "I learned a bit of the game, and I came to like it. But the nuances, there are so many."

"Yes," Collins said. "And those nuances might be changing."

"What do you mean?" Daugava asked.

"Doctor, I would like to talk to you about a position with the NPL. I would like you to fly to New York. I can assure you the job would embrace your scientific know-how, and not test you on the rules and particulars about football."

Daugava then heard Collins' proposal and slowly smiled. After a few minutes of listening, he thanked the commissioner and said goodbye, then put down the phone. He stared at Rotinom, the large figure laying peacefully on a work table with the doctor's multitude of tools hanging on an adjacent work bench.

Collins put down the phone in his office and picked up a folder marked TASK FORCE: RR. Under that heading a mission statement was typed, a paragraph about a possible solution to reduce the number of concussions and injuries in football. A short list of names was listed, the first one being "Daugava, consultant."

He had begun outlining his plan as soon as the league's board decided the years of service and leadership from Collins outweighed his tenure as commissioner during "Rigagate," as it became known. Instead of disavowing robots, Collins went in the opposite direction. He created the task force to consider whether each team should have one 'Rotinom' play for it. He would couch the idea as a way to reduce injuries, but in the end it would be about a lot more than that. Robots didn't go to bars and get drunk and miss games. They didn't pack guns in duffel bags and try to check them at an airport. They didn't hit officials. Machines didn't get hurt or become ill. And, perhaps most important to the league office and team owners, they weren't temperamental when negotiating salaries.

In his Cleveland apartment, Daugava stood quietly for a moment.

"Well, Riga, it seems your career in this sport might not be completely finished," he said aloud. With that, he went to pack for the trip to New York.

Riga Rotinom didn't make it through the season, but that didn't mean his career was over.

ACKNOWLEDGMENTS

Years ago—I think I was in my teens—my father turned to me and said, "You know what I'd like to see? A story about this great football player. And at the end of the day…" Thus was born the idea for this book. So **Jack Bona** gets the first hat tip.

My sister **Mia Bonavoglia** is not the world's biggest sports fan, but she always brings a keen eye to my writing, making sure I don't overstate or understate anything. If I do, I can be sure of a deft editor's touch as well as a humorous admonishment.

My mother **Yole Bona** instilled in me a love of reading with many trips to public libraries when I was young. Those treks were special then, and I still value them.

I sought out several talented editors at various stages to read this book. Should the reader find mistakes, I take full blame. These are the people who saved me from embarrassing mistakes:

Samantha Farlow and I first worked together in Gary, Indiana, in the late 1990s. It didn't take long to see she was an editing talent. She moved on to The Plain Dealer in Cleveland and then the New York Times. She took the first edit on this book, and I can't thank her enough for bringing together her sports knowledge and editing ability. She put as much attention and passion into reading this as she does in being a New York Yankees fan.

Having a colleague like **Bob Higgs**—a reporter, editor and lawyer—is invaluable. I can't count the times I have called on him with legal advice. He took a read on this book and, as usual, came through with immediate clarity.

William "Skip" Hall, a sports copy editor at The Plain Dealer, was named Ohio's Headline Writer of the Year in 2018 by the Associated Press Media Editors. Skip makes a living catching mistakes on a frantic nightly deadline, and he was a natural choice to edit my work.

My wife, **Lynne Sherwin**, is a talented editor who takes a common-sense approach and asks stupid questions as often as she cooks a bad meal—which is to say, never.

Over the years, I have followed, read and written about, covered, edited and, of course, watched a lot of football at multiple levels. I thought I had a good understanding of the game until I met legendary Northeast Ohio football coach **John Piai**. He was gracious enough and patient to meet me for a cup of coffee in the snowy dead of winter to give me his perspective from years of coaching. And while I did not base the coach in this book on him, I gleaned so much knowledge.

Speaking of coaches: I covered University of Iowa football during my college years, and the part about the pink lockers is based on Kinnick Stadium's visiting locker room. **Hayden Fry** was a hoot to cover, and it's no surprise national television broadcasts trot out footage of the pink urinals every season.

My brother-in-law **Bob Sherwin** is a master of puns, and several of his found their way into these pages. I am grateful for his sense of humor and his generosity for letting me use them.

I am fortunate to know many talented artists who cover a range of styles. **Kathy Hagedorn** was the first person I thought to approach for the cover design of "The Game Changer." While a character's true image is in the mind's eye of the reader, I feel her images fit the characters wonderfully.

Fellow writers **Scott Longert** and **Bob Adamov** were quick to accept my requests to pick their brains. Their advice on navigating the publishing world remains invaluable.

I have worked in daily newspapers and now the digital side of reporting, writing and editing. I have seen women get shut out of lockers, and I have watched as the doors slowly crept open. The reporter in this book is not based on any one person, nor is she a compilation. My hope is that she is considered a small homage to any woman in the business, especially those who reported on sports in the 1980s.

—MARC BONA

ABOUT THE AUTHOR

Marc Bona is an award-winning features writer for cleveland. com who previously worked in assorted editing roles for *The Plain Dealer* in Cleveland, *The Post-Tribune* in Gary, Indiana; *The Times Union* in Albany, New York; *The Detroit News, San Antonio Light* and *The Dallas Morning News*. He lives in Akron, Ohio, with his wife Lynne Sherwin and rescue pup, Addie. He can be reached at mbona30@neo.rr.com.

A portion of the sales from this book will go to two Northeast Ohio-based charities: Shoes and Clothes for Kids in Cleveland (sc4k.org) and Good Samaritan Hunger Center in Akron (goodsamaritanhungercenter.org).